Records c

MW01487006

Records of the Transmission of the Lamp

(Jingde Chuandeng Lu)

by
Daoyuan

edited by
Yang Yi

Translated from the Original Chinese
by
Randolph S. Whitfield

Volume I
(Books 1-3)
The Buddhas and Indian Patriarchs

景德傳燈錄

Records of the Transmission of the Lamp
Up to the Era of Great Virtue [of the Song Dynasty CE 1004-7]

(Jap: Keitoku Dentōroku)

Compiled by
Daoyuan

of the Chan School, of the later Song Dynasty
in 30 fascicules.

© 2015 Randolph Whitfield
Artwork by Buch&media GmbH, München
Cover design by Sandra Hill. Detail from the image
of Avalokitesvara leading a lady to the Pure Land, from the Dunhuang Caves.
Courtesy of the Trustees of the British Museum, London.
Printed by BoD – Books on Demand
Printed in Germany
ISBN 978-3-7386-6246-7

Fragrance
of the
Dharma

Hōkun Trust

Contents

Preface

The scale of the present translation is so big (more volumes are to follow) that I have taken the interests of the general reader as my main concern. A fully annotated translation of the *Jingde Chuandeng Lu* 景德傳燈錄 (Records of the Transmission of the Lamp, hereafter CDL) would necessarily comprise many more additional volumes, yet with Buddhism being so new in the West copious annotations to a work of this scale would only be a distraction from the main work itself, although such annotations certainly promise to be a fruitful voyage of discovery in the future. Neither is the introduction written in the style of an academic discourse. It is too early for such a presentation and too limiting for such a complex subject. This is the first complete translation of the primary canonical text of the Chinese Chan School[1] and will surely benefit from a detailed exegesis one day: but first of all it needs to be appreciated in its entirety.

With regard to the Chan Buddhist milieu we are on a very slow boat to China. Happily the literature on Song Dynasty Buddhism and its complex history is growing apace, so there are many fine books on the background to this most interesting subject.[2]

This Chinese work has never been completely translated into any language except modern Chinese. It is a collection of Buddhist biographies, teaching and transmission stories of Indian and Chinese Chan (Japanese 'Zen') masters from antiquity up to about the year 1008 CE. What makes this collection so remarkable is that it is the first mature fruit of an already thousand year-long spiritual marriage between two great world cultures with quite different ways of viewing the world. The fertilisation of Chinese spirituality by Indian Buddhism not only fructified the Chinese civilisation, but the whole Asian culture field, as well as extending far west to the Mediterranean basin even in early times.

---

[1] Discounting the *Zutang Ji* 祖堂集 (The Anthology from the Patriarchal Hall) which might possibly be a product of Korean Chan, not Chinese.

[2] Regarding the CDL, see Albert Welter, *Monks, Rulers, and Literati: The Political Ascendancy of Chan Buddhism.* Oxford, 2006 (MRL), and Wittern, Christian. *Das Yulu des Chan-Buddhismus: Die Entwicklung vom 8.-11. Jahrhundert am Beispiel des 28. Kapitels des Jingde chuandeng lu (1004).* Bern, 1998 (YCB), and Christian Wittern, *Jingde chuandeng lu. Aufzeichnungen von der Übertragung der Leuchte aus der Ära Jingde* (AUL). Insel Verlag, Suhrkamp, 2014 , which contains selections from the CDL.

The message to which this work gives expression was made accessible by the political and literary skill of Chinese redactors in the retelling of records, old stories and legends culled from rich and various sources both oral and written.

Randolph S. Whitfield

Acknowledgements

In gratitude to the Venerable Myokyoni of London who pointed out the way of Master Linji (Rinzai) for many years.

Thanks to the Hokun Trust of London for granting funds for this translation and its publication.

Thanks to the Venerable Sohaku Ogata, whose work continues.

Thanks to Carman Blacker for her far-sightedness.

Thanks to the Ven. Myokun of The Hermitage of the True Dharma (Shobo-an) London, for real enthusiasm and practical help.

Thanks to Michelle Bromley for much practical help and encouragement, without which this book would never have come into being.

Last but not least, thanks go to my wife Mariana, who has supported me all along the Way.

Introduction

The Way to the Heart

The knowledge of what we are as human beings and of where we have come from still resembles somewhat one of our medieval maps. The known territory that has been drawn out is very small, not accurately scaled down or projected, whilst physical experience still tells us that the world is flat. Likewise, the known part of our human nature is extremely small too, still being confined to a familiarity with mechanics or to that part of us which is cognisant. The 'unused ninety percent', as the common figure has it, is vast uncharted space into which few have ventured alive and most fear to tread.

If we remain so unknown to ourselves, is there any hope of finding the happiness we are all looking for? If man's treasure lies where his Heart is (the repeated message in these biographies), then the treasure must be right under our very noses. Perhaps it is like Father Christmas and his Tree, the focal point at Christmas where the ritual of faith is renewed and strengthened, the living proof of our natural capacity for joy. We want to be uplifted, as proved by being disappointed every year by religious holidays that fail to fulfil the longings for a deeper delight. Ritual might be a safe haven from all that dark space, but is a safe entrance to it as well; it is the container which confines, restrains and tempers the mighty flow of Nature's raw impersonal passion which fills us all to the brim.

Buddhism is based on a spiritual 'practice of relativity' applicable in any life situation. Quite simply the practice functions as if everything were related to everything else. Straightforward enough one might think, yet the practice seems to cause peculiar difficulties on our home-world. Relativity means that every thing, state, level, dimension or phenomenon whatever is related to every other such as to totally preclude even the idea that there could exist something that is a closed, self-sufficient system within itself, without relations to its surroundings. Superficially this seems simple enough but it is the far-reaching implications of such teachings that cause the most trouble, the foremost being the obvious deduction that if everything is related to everything else, then there cannot exist a self-subsisting essence of any kind that could be called an independent, nuclear, permanent Self. Only an entity that has no relationship with anything outside of itself could be said to be self-sufficient. If such a thing is radically inconceivable then the inevitable conclusion to draw from this truth is that an individual unchanging permanent essence does not exist. There is the deed, but no unchanging agent who does the doing. It is this which causes so much trouble, for although we feel ourselves to be nuclear entities within our own right, the plain fact of a sojourn in a particular life situation only too clearly shows that the feeling is entirely illusory. As shown, for example, by the inconvenient evidence of the very termination of a particular life situation, a termination over which there is usually no control and which is therefore feared more than anything else. Any truly self-sufficient, nuclear entity would have total control over all the processes of its closed systemic self-existence and over the circumstances of its own termination. An outside force would have absolutely no influence over it. Yet we can't even choose not to have a headache!

Life is the arena, the live theatre of action, executed in a particular mode conformable to environment and circumstances. The 'game' in this arena seems to be based on inter-action, for the mutual enrichment, benefit, joy and sorrow of all of us, the centre of the relativity truth. It is the whole environment that benefits from every member engaging wholeheartedly in it, that is, of being alive in this absolute relativity.

The ancient Indians had a wonderfully sensitive word for 'relativity', applied in its deepest meaning. The term preserved its inviolability even on its later journey to the west, by virtue of being anyway untranslatable. Perhaps that is why the original word has gained a foothold even in our Western culture, with the prospect of becoming a universal term, understood by all yet fully explainable by none: 'Dharma'. Temporarily bound together, all things are related with each other, as the spokes of a wheel are related to the hub and *vice versa*, all bound together by the rim.[3]

Dharma is an ancient word coined by the Indian religious genius, matured by uncommon powers of introversion and its spin-off, the development of complex memory systems, the route by which the Buddhist *Suttas*[4] of Buddha Shakyamuni have come down to us. With the spiritual techniques acquired

---

[3] Dharma with a capital 'D' in this translation usually connotes the principle of relativity in this sense; whilst small 'd' dharma denotes a thing and whatever it is temporarily related to; but I have been unable to be consistent in this usage due to the complexity of the Chinese text.

[4] *Suttas* – the books of the Buddhist canon in which the words of Buddha Shakyamuni are reported.

through meditation, the Indians mapped a way to the hierarchies of 'the Gods and Goddesses' working in man, earthbound in his case of flesh, with a precision not found in any other terrestrial culture. Arising from the urge to bring insight to consciousness there arose a technical vocabulary of great analytical acumen to serve as the vehicle for the data of this knowledge.

The Ancient Chinese, on the other hand, were not given to religion in the Indian sense of the word. Confucius 孔子 (551-476 BCE), a contemporary of Pythagoras (578-510 BCE) and Buddha (c.563-483 BCE), was not in the least interested in the question of whether Gods existed or not, of whether or not there was an afterlife (neither was Buddha for that matter). The Chinese were interested in the concrete objective world, in the knowable, above all in the human being and in cultivating his harmonious relations in this life.[5] The immediate *family* hierarchy natural to the kinship unit was therefore very important to them and this structure was the paradigm for governing village, county, prefecture, district, province and Empire.[6] The head of state was the Ruler (*wang* 王), his 'sons' the immediate ministers, and relatives governed the provinces. Although the Ruler was a father to his people, he was also a son, called 'the Son of Heaven'. The structure of the kinship unit was also seen in the visible heavenly bodies: the sun was the father, the orbiting planets his minister-sons, the star systems the in-laws. The Son of Heaven stood in the middle, the intermediary between Heaven and Earth, representing Man the great being. Veneration of ancestors by the Chinese was the reverencing of this all-encompassing natural order, which needed no proof of its reality because it is for all to see. Most important for the maintenance of this order were two particular qualities

---

[5] See the *Li Ji* (Book of Rites), chapter 31, translated by Séraphin Couvreur in *Mémoires sur les Bienséances et les Cérémonies, Tome* II. Leiden: Brill, 1950, p. 463, section 25, on the Chinese ideal of self-cultivation and the putting of it to use for the benefit of others. Also known as *The Doctrine of the Mean*, (translated into English by James Legge, Oxford, 1893) it was later to be taken up by the Neo-Confucianists as a basic text.

[6] 'However frequent they were, the ceremonies of the great cults in the domanial towns did not exhaust religious activity. Even if we ignore a multitude of ritual acts performed in honour of deities of place and occasion – those performed in passing through a door, getting into a chariot, eating vegetables in season – we can say that the daily life of a noble was spent wholly in religious exercises: such were the exercises imposed by filial piety or the fealty of vassals, for father and lord possessed a Majesty nurtured by continuous homage.' Granet, Marcel, *The Religion of the Chinese People*. Blackwell, p.90.

peculiar to humans: *ren* 仁 and *yi* 義, benevolence and moral purity.[7] The Ruler received his mandate to rule from heaven on account of his outstanding qualities of *ren* and *yi*. The individual is solely responsible for the cultivation of both these qualities by virtue of them being inherent in man.[8]

Although the Ancient Chinese were a down to earth people they also had another side to them for they possessed many categories of sorcerers, sorceresses, mediums, exorcists, rainmakers and other occultists,[9] whose knowledge was usually put to use in practical arts such as the way of good government, good medicine or even astrology as an aid to a better life. Knowledge of the energies (spirits) inhabiting the human body and their relationship with astral coefficients (divinities) were the basis for health regimes.[10] The Daoist *yuren* 羽人 (feather-man) Shaman, for example, was not subject to possession but was a master who had learnt to navigate his way through the spiritual realms[11] into the deathless. Already in the 'Songs from Chu' (*Chuci* 楚辭), a classic collection of Chinese poetry from the 4th century BCE, there are many examples of shamanic procedures and religious songs.

In later times the life of a certain Tao Hongjing 陶弘景 (451-536 CE) is paradigmatic of the interpenetration of the different realms of activity common to the Chinese cultural elite from early times on: their perennial search for cultural continuity through learning, their search for immortality through the practice of meditation techniques, and the invocation of spiritual forces for the preservation of a conservative society governed by sagely policies. Before Tao's birth his mother dreamt that a green dragon issued from her bosom[12] and that

---

[7] *Ren* and *yi* are both insights central to the teaching of Mencius, a Confucian sage almost as venerable as Confucius himself. See the interesting article in *Three Ways of Thought in Ancient China* by Arthur Waley, 1939, Stanford reprint, 1983. pp. 83-145. Mencius is in Penguin Classics, translated by D.C.Lau, 1970.

[8] See *Lunyu* 論語 (*Analects of Confucius*), XII.1, etc. There are many translations of this classic.

[9] Mircea Eliade, *Shamanism: Archaic Techniques of Ecstasy.* Harmondsworth reprint, 1989, p.450.

[10] See Edward H. Shafer, *Mirages on the Sea of Time: The Taoist Poetry of T'sao T'ang.* University of California Press, 1985, p.6.

[11] Berthold Laufer, *The Pre-History of Aviation.* Field Museum of Natural History (Chicago), Anthropological Series XVIII.I, 1928, p.26.

[12] The viscera had their corresponding animals in Chinese Daoist medicinal lore, liver-dragon, lungs-tiger, heart-red bird, spleen-phoenix, kidneys-stag and sometimes gall-

two spiritual beings came to her house, holding in their hands a bronze censer.[13] He was an eccentric child, grew up handsome and very tall, an omnivorous reader and skilled performer on the lute. When still young Tao wanted to find the secret of immortality and before manhood was appointed by Emperor Gao 高帝 (r. 479-483 CE) of the Qi齊 dynasty to be tutor to the Imperial Princes. But in 492 he resigned and went to live in the mountains as a Daoist recluse, calling himself 'the hermit of Huayang' (*huayang yinshi* 華陽隱士). He built a three storey tower, lived on the top floor and had his pupils live in the middle whilst visitors were received on the ground floor. Among his visitors was the renowned future Buddhist Emperor Wu of the Liang dynasty, who offered Tao a ministerial post on his accession to the throne. Tao declined but Emperor Wu would consult him from time to time, from which he earned the sobriquet 'Minister in the Mountains' (*shanzhong zaixiang)* 山中宰相). He passed a long life in alchemical studies, practising breathing techniques and trying to live without food (a common enough practice amongst adepts in those days) and his favourite delight was listening to the breeze blowing through the mountain pines. He made his contribution to *wen* 文 (culture, see below) by authoring a work on the manufacture of famous swords (*Daojian Lu* 刀 尖 錄) and won immortality for himself through his *Materia Medica* containing a description of some 370 medicinal plants,[14] the *Mingyi Bielu* 名 醫 別 錄 (*Miscellaneous Records of Famous Physicians*), still in use today. To cap it all he invented an elixir (*fei tan* 非 丹), made only of gold, cinnabar, azurite and sulphur, materials supplied by the Emperor, who tasted it and awarded its manufacture.[15] Apart from Tao Hongjing's influence on the Buddhist Emperor Wu of Liang, he is perhaps best remembered as the greatest writer on Daoism of his day: he edited the whole corpus of writings left by the founders of the *Shangqing* 上青 (Supreme

bladder-turtle-snake. I.P. Couliano, *Out of this World*. Shambhala, 1991, p. 75. See also the remark by Kaptchuk, 'Chinese medicine is a coherent system of thought that does not require validation by the West as an intellectual construct.' Ted J. Kaptchuk, *Chinese Medicine: The Web that has no Weaver*. Rider, 2000, p.77.

[13] I follow Giles, CBD: 1896 for these biographical details.

[14] 'The Chinese…are better informed on the history of important plants than any other people in Asia (and I should even venture to add, of Europe)…' *Sino-Iranica*: 'Chinese Contributions to the History of Civilization in Ancient Iran', by Berthold Laufer, Field Museum of Natural History no. 201 Vol. XV, no.3, Chicago, 1919, p. 204.

[15] B. Laufer, *The Pre-History of Aviation*. Chicago, 1928, p. 29, cited in Couliano, I.P., *Out of this World*. Shambhala, 1991, p.72.

Clarity) School of Daoism, systemised their doctrines and brought order to their protean mythologies. Shangqing was the school of Daoism favoured by the Emperors and the literate class for more than 300 years (960-1279).[16] Such illustrious men are not rare in Chinese history.

[16] Cahill, Suzanne E., *Transcendence and Divine Passion: The Queen Mother of the West in Medieval China*. Stanford, 1993, pp. 32-35.

The Central Asian Roundabout

Although China and India are old neighbours, the Himalayan Mountains and the Tibetan Plateau separate them geographically. Their more intimate religious courtship only began seriously around the beginning of the Christian era and took place on the neutral, or at least, disputed ground of 'Central Asia'.

The Tarim Basin is a vast and ancient depression in the modern Xinjiang-Uygur region of China's far west, extending 900 miles east to west and up to 300 miles north to south. The Celestial Terrace Mountains (Tianshan 天山[17]) enclose this Central Asian roundabout to the north-west, the Kunlun Mountains 昆侖山 [18] to the south and the Pamirs to the west; the east end is the open Gansu corridor to China. The major part of the Basin is occupied by the extensive sandy desert known as the Taklamakan, but two chains of oases, on the north rim and south rim, link the east end with the west end of the Tarim Basin. These two routes, called the Silk Road, were the meeting places of all the peoples of Asia. This huge roundabout,[19] busy throughout recorded history, had four exits: west to the Hellenic world and the Mediterranean, south to the Indian sub-continent, north to the Steppe lands of the nomads and east to China.

The northern rim of the Silk Road went from Dunhuang, a staging post in China's far west and continued west through the oases of Shorchu, Turfan, Kucha and Aksu to Kashgar and further to Samarkand in the east. The southern chain of oases, also starting from Dunhuang and going west were Miran, Charchan, Niya, Keriya, Khotan, Yarkand, Kashgar, then to Herat and Kabul in the south-west. A wide variety of languages were spoken along these two routes – Altaic speakers such as the Xiongnu, Turks, Uighurs, Mongols; the Sino-Tibetan speakers – Chinese, Tibetans, Tanguts and Indo-European speakers from Kucha, Khota and Sogdia.[20] The manu-

---

[17] Also a famous Buddhist pilgrimage centre.

[18] A sacred place to the Ancient Chinese where lived Xi Wangmu, the Queen Mother of the West. See Cahill, Suzanne E., *The Queen Mother of the West in Medieval China*. Stanford, pp, 18-19 and below.

[19] The concept of the 'Central Asian Roundabout' was Arnold Toynbee's. See *A Study of History'*, (SH) Vol. V: 140 & XI: map 21b.

[20] See *Buddhism in Central Asia* by B.N. Puri. Dehli: Motilal Banarsidass,1987, Rprt. 1993, p.17ff, for a treatment of the ancient routes.

scripts found in 1900 by Sir Aurel Stein at the eastern exit of this roundabout, near Dunhuang, reveal its cosmopolitan character, whose control was disputed by all these peoples throughout history.[21] Sinic domination here was an off-and-on affair. The courtship between the Chinese and a brand of Indic Buddhism newly emerging in this Central Asian melting pot was of course a result of the vicissitudes in the relations between all these contending peoples, but a new Buddhism was brought into this area from Northern India by the originally nomadic Kushans,[22] who had built an Empire stretching from the Aral to the Arabian Sea that included Northern India and Kashmir to the south, Khotan in the northeast, Greek Bactria and Parthia in the northwest. The Kushan Empire, which took its inspiration from Hellenic, Iranian and Indian sources, built the cultural bridge between India in the south and China to the east, by facilitating mutual trade.

The attraction pulling from both sides of the bridge, with the Kushans as the middle-men, was very complex, for on the surface the Chinese and Indians seemed poles apart temperamentally. The Indian was completely at home in the doctrines of *karman* (actions) and rebirth (consequences) and in the cyclic development of universes reckoned in aeons (*kalpas*). The Chinese seemed primarily interested in applying their equally formidable gifts to the concrete here and now – health, farming, weather forecasting and maintaining political security in a world of predators. Being neighbours since ancient times there had been some hybridisation, but the courtship proper started at the beginning of the Christian era when the Chinese first came to hear of an Indian sage already famous on their sub-continent for some four hundred years, the Buddha Shakyamuni.

A lot of initial adjustments had to be made to welcome this alien religion onto Chinese soil. First from India came Buddhism in its Hinayāna (traditional) form and only later came the Mahāyāna (developed) form.[23] This proved fortuitous since Traditional Buddhism's chief concern was with Man and the curing of his ills, a true humanism appealing to the practical cast of the Chinese mentality.[24] In order to make sense of the foreign religion, traditional Chinese concepts rooted in their native Daoism and philosophy was the means of effecting an initial syn-

---

[21] HCC: 19.
[22] SH: V, 139-147.
[23] The Kushans were carriers of Hinayāna Buddhism and of the new religion of Mahāyāna, still in gestation at the turn of the Christian era.
[24] See SH: IX. 42.

cretism.[25] An apologetic literature arose quite early that often took the form of a dialogue between author (host, *zhu*主) and an imaginary opponent (guest, *bin*賓), the challenger finally declaring himself convinced of some strange new concept.[26]

The early attraction the Chinese had for the Indian Mauryan King Aśoka (c.270-230 BCE)[27] was an indicator of their perennial concern for the art of governance and of religion put to the service of the state. This earlier Indian empire builder was famous for his faith in the Hinayāna Buddhist religion and for his rock edicts, admonishing non-violence, tolerance and devotion to *Dhamma*.[28] Aśoka was also the subject of legend – in his zeal to convert the whole of India to the Buddhist faith, he had relics of the Buddha housed in 84,000 *stupas*, erected over the whole of his Empire. The legend, presented as history in the *Aśokarājāvadāna*,[29] was eagerly taken up later by the Chinese to serve as an example of a good 'Son of Heaven'. The Chinese even became convinced, during the third and fourth centuries CE, that Aśoka's universal rule of six hundred years before must also have included China in its orbit at that time. If Buddhism had been native to Chinese soil – so the argument went – it was only a question of finding the remains of Aśoka's *stupas* to verify this.[30] A relic cult arose as a result. Indeed, sometime between 373-376 CE a Chinese monk by the name of Huida 'discovered' the Buddha's hair and fingernails preserved in a golden casket buried at the base of a *stupa* in Jiangkang (present Nanjing) and it was determined that the find came out of one of the stupas that Aśoka had built. Later Emperor Wu of Liang (r. 502-549 CE), the famous *Chinese* Buddhist Emperor and friend of Tao Hongjing, rebuilt the *stupa* at Nanjing and lavishly venerated the relic there.[31]

[25] BCC: 11-13.
[26] This literature is mostly contained in *Hongming Ji* 弘明記 ('The Collection of Great Clarifications'), T. 2102, compiled by Sengyou 僧祐between 515-518 CE and *Guang Hongming Ji* 廣弘明記('The Extended Collection of Great Clarifications'), T. 2103, compiled by Daoxuan 道玄in 664. See BCC: 13. See also *A History of Chinese Philosophy* by Fung Yu-lan. Princeton, 1953, 1973, pp. 272-274, for some translated passages.
[27] A good treatment of King Aśoka and his reign is to be found in HIB: 223-259.
[28] A translation of the Edicts of Asoka can be found in *Asoka and the Decline of the Mauryas* by Romila Thapar. Oxford University Press, 1961. *Dhamma* is Pali for Dharma.
[29] A Study and translation of the Aśokāvadāna was made by John Strong, *The Legend of King Aśoka*. See also *The Heavenly Exploits: Biographies from the Divyāvadāna*, translated by Joel Tatleman. Clay Sanskrit Library. The Chinese translation is in T. 2042.
[30] BCC: 277ff.
[31] BDT: 61.

Such legends already helped to give a legitimacy and pedigree to the Imperial prestige.[32] Trade in relics became big business later and the means of continental travel: merchants and monks of various nationalities travelled between India and China in search of texts and relics, along the well-trodden Silk Road.

The Kushans were Indo-European nomads of the *Yuezhi*月支 people and had already invaded North-west India in the 1st century of our era, after overcoming the Greeks, Sakas (a Scythian people) and Parthians. The famous and devout Kushan Buddhist King, Kaniṣka (2nd century CE) had multiple relations with kingdoms to the east and west[33] – there is ample numismatic evidence of trade relations with Rome, Egypt, Central Asia and China [34] – and had the great Buddhist Saint Aśvagosha as an ornament to his court.[35] The spiritual assimilation of a developing, itinerant Indian Buddhism coming out of the Indus Valley and coming into contact with the Chinese world through the medium of the Kushan Empire owed much to the great Kaniṣka. His adoption of sophisticated Mahāyāna doctrines, especially of the *Madhyamika* (Middle Way) School, which espoused the radical teaching of the 'no self-nature' of all things (śūnyatā), propounded by the semi-legendary sage Nāgārjuna (c. 150-250 CE), perhaps known to Kaniṣka's court too, gave the Chinese quite a headache when it first arrived on Sinic soil, but bore fruit from around the 5th century onwards.[36]

---

[32] BCC: 280.

[33] For the interchange of ideas between India and Greece see, from the Indian side, the *Milindapanha* ('Questions of King Milinda) in various translations. From the Greek side, see the Travel Records of Apollonius of Tyana, a famous Neopythagorean sage born at the beginning of the Christian era and much given to the life of an ascetic wandering teacher, even reaching India; often compared with his contemporary, Jesus of Nazareth (see *Life of Apollonius* by Philostratus, trsl. by F.C. Conybeare, Loeb Classical Library*).* See also *Ta Indika* by Megathenes (c. 350-290 BCE) for an early account of India, the travels of an ambassador sent by Seleucus I to the court of the Indian king, Chandragupta, founder of the Mauryas.

[34] Examined in Tarn, W.W., *The Greeks in Bactria and India.* Cambridge University Press, 1938, pp. 503-7, following Toynbee, *A Study of History,* Vol. V. p.133, n.1.

[35] See a recent PhD thesis entitled 'Conceiving the Indian Buddhist Patriarchs in China' by Stuart H. Young. Princeton 2008, for a treatment of Aśvagoṣa, father of the Mahāyāna, and other Indian Patriarchs.

[36] The first great translator of Indian Buddhist texts into Chinese, Kumārajīva 鳩摩羅什 answers eighteen letters by Huiyuan 惠遠 the eminent Chinese Buddhist, writ-

The wholesale adoption of Indian Buddhism by the Sinic world, first in the form of the Hinayāna of King Aśoka followed by the eclectic Mahāyānaism of King Kaniṣka, was effected with the greatest intensity over a long period of time and reached its first high point during the Tang dynasty (618-906 CE) in China.[37] The adoption appeared complete only with the absence of Indian originals in the rapidly growing indigenous Chinese Buddhist literature, flowering under the hands of literati-editors in the Song dynasty (960-1278 CE).The process would fructify the whole of the Asian culture field for centuries.

ten between 405 and 409 CE, collected and edited between 470 and 600 under the title *Dasheng Dayi Zhang* (Compendium on the Great Purport of the Mahayana) in T.1856. See BCC: 226ff. for overview and fuller translation in Robinson, Richard H. *Early Mādhyamika in India and China.* Madison, 1967, pp. 177-317. For a translation of the Gao Seng Zhuan biography of Kumārajīva by Huijiao (T.50, 2059) see Nobel, Johannes, 'Kumārajīva' in *Sitzungsberichte der Preussischen Akademie der Wissenschaften,* Philosophisch-Historische Klasse, Jahrgang 1927. Berlin, 1927.

[37] Imperial patronage played an important role in the growth of Buddhist Schools in the Tang. See 'Imperial Patronage in T'ang Buddhism' by Stanley Weinstein, pp. 265-307, in *Perspectives on the Tang,* Edited by Arthur F. Wright and Denis Twitchett. Yale, 1973.

The Song Awakening

If the best literatures are the repositories of the insights and wisdom of a culture, according to time and place on the one hand, but embracing eternal verities on the other, then 'eternal verities' most likely express the communality of the human nature, fairly standard in all places and in all times. To the Chinese, the impulse to go back to the ancient repositories enshrined in the records of *bona fide* teachers is natural, as is the recording of new lessons and insights for the sake of posterity. It is seen as a sacred duty to do this, not merely a political expedient.

Just as the Indians have the word 'Dharma', so the Chinese also have their word *wen* 文 whose primary definition is 'literature' or 'writing'. It is very difficult for a non-Chinese to conceive of the importance of literature in the life of China through the ages. *Wen* is the lifeline to the richly composed wisdom gained from millennia of recording political experience within the tableau of the cosmological backdrop, of literary discussions on the contents of these records, all used in a practical way as the nutrient to the exercise of wise statecraft. *Wen* fertilised the art of governance as a continuous process.

There have been many flowerings of *wen* in the history of China, for it signifies not only literature but by extension, 'culture'. In Song 宋 times (c. 960-1279 CE) the development of the art of woodblock printing in the 10th and 11th century contributed more than anything else to a spectacular literary renaissance that continued well into the fourteenth. Woodblock printing must have had about the same effect on the dissemination of information as the Internet and the cell phone is having on our world today. The Song Emperors were quick to pursue a policy of printing standard texts as a means of popularising the uniqueness of the Chinese, that is, Song culture. Literature now meant stability, continuity and modernity. The variety of works published was impressive – the Confucian classics, texts on mathematics, medicine, agriculture, warfare, codes of law, philosophy, vast dynastic histories – and collections of Daoist and Buddhist literature.[38]

---

[38] The first complete collection of Buddhist works (Tripitaka), printed in the city of Chengdu, Sichuan Province, SW China was the Shuban edition, of 5,586 fascicles. There were at least six separate printings of the Buddhist Tripitaka during the Song, starting in 971 CE with the Kaibao Zangshu 開寶藏書 in 1076 fascicles. It took ten

It was the first time in world history that there had been so much to read by so many.[39]

The Northern Song period, from around 960 to the 1120's, was an exciting, if rather turbulent time, bringing a complete transformation of political, social and economic life. The old Tang dynasty statecraft ideals of a uniform rule for the whole empire had given way to the decentralisation of a government ruled by bureaucrats. Prosperous local power bases arose as a result so that a redistribution of the population took place, a movement from the predominantly populated north to the central and southern regions. Within this new milieu a free market developed in land and urban centres became areas of growth and prosperity, ushering in a new breed of entrepreneurs, the merchant class. On the coast, the ports were active too, for one of the most important phenomenon in Asian history was taking place at the same time – the Chinese maritime expansion of the eleventh century. From the ports of Fujian, Zhejiang and Guangdong great ocean-going junks capable of accommodating a thousand people were plying the seas from Japan to Arabia.

The price of all this development however was that the non-Chinese surrounding the great Middle Kingdom (中國 China) – Khitans, Tanguts and Jurchens – wanted to have a slice of the prosperity, whilst those on the inside, especially local commanders and bureaucrats, would become weak from too much good living and too little vigilance. But these were heady days; society was transforming and there was an expanding money economy.[40] In 1024 rich merchants and financiers in Chengdu, Sichuan province, even issued certificates of deposit, the precursors of banknotes. But Song China was surround-

years to cut the 130,000 woodblocks for this edition and was not surpassed in size until the Ming dynasty. See *Chinese History: A Manual* by Endymion Porter Wilkinson. Harvard Yenching Institute, 2000, p.450.

[39] 'In the execution of the preliminary task of collecting, editing, annotating, and publishing the surviving works of a "dead" classical literature, the Far Eastern emperors of a resuscitated Sinic universal state had not only far outdistanced all their competitors up to date but had raised paper monuments whose pyramid-like mass could not easily have been equalled even by the output of a post-Modern Western World with its unprecedented capacity for material production', Arnold Toynbee, SH: IX. 53. (Toynbee was wrong, of course, to label classical Chinese as a 'dead' language, since all the characters of that language, with more or less the same semantic values, are still in use)

[40] The issue of coins in strings of 1000 shot up from 270,000 in 995 CE to an astounding 1,350,000 in 1000 CE, peaking at 6,000,000 in 1073. HCC: 325.

ed – the Uigurs had already set up an empire in the Tarim Basin during the 840's, the Khitan, a Mongolian speaking people, had founded the Liao dynasty in the north China area in 947.[41] At the beginning of the 11th century the Liao launched victorious battles in Hubei and Shaanxi provinces culminating in an ignominious peace treaty (Peace of Shanyuan in 1004) by which the Song undertook to pay a heavy annual tribute, increased in 1042.[42] Then the Jurchen, ancestors of the future Manchu rulers, overthrew the Liao dynasty and occupied the whole of north China in 1126. The Khitan set up a western Liao in east Turkestan, whilst the Jurchen founded the Jin dynasty from 1122. In the northwest of China the Tanguts, Tibetan speakers, founded the kingdom of Xixia, which encroached on the old Han provinces of Shaanxi, Shanxi and Gansu, from 1038 until 1227. The Xia threat grew worse so that the government had to take emergency measures, calling on Minister Wang Anshi 王安石 (1021-86), armed with plenary powers, to put into effect a whole series of radical reforms. But he alienated the big land owners and rich merchants, was removed from office and replaced by Sima Guang 司馬光 (1019-86).

The arts chronicled the renaissance. Chinese canons of painting became firmly established during the Song, reaching a level of perfection rarely achieved in later dynasties. Monochrome, impressionistic landscape painting was more important than the previous Tang emphasis on figure painting. The ferment and energy of this period is masterfully depicted in the famous 12th century, five-metre long monochrome silk scroll painting (the *Qingming Shanghe Tu* 清明上河圖) only found in 1954 in the Beijing Palace Museum. It shows the great metropolis of Kaifeng (Henan) during the spring festival, busy with people on the streets, great barges on the river, tea houses, shops, restaurants, street

---

[41] The Liao were nomadic cattle breeders in the modern Manchurian area of north China. The Liao founded a dynasty in the 10th century which was only destroyed in 1218 by Genghis Khan. They were in contact with Japan to the east and the Abassid Caliphate to the west. Khitan (another name for the Liao, which was to become 'Cathay' to Marco Polo) princesses were sought by the court of Baghdad. Their adopted religion was also Buddhism – they published their own Tripitaka (based on the Shu edition) in 1055. The Buddhist religion and Liao's exposure to Chinese culture seems to have had a fatal effect on its martial spirit. HCC: 351-4.

[42] The tribute imposed on the Song and fixed at the Peace of Shanyuan as 100,000 ounces of silver and 200,000 rolls of silk per year, was raised in 1042 to 200,000 ounces of silver and 300,000 rolls of silk in consideration of the help given by the Liao dynasty to the Song in its struggles against the Tangut. HCC: 353.

vendors and bookshops, the whole scene bustling with a life not much different from any metropolis today.[43]

In literature, not only were many standard works printed for the first time but new genres were gaining respectability. Novels and the popular theatre were increasingly in vogue, for both reflected ordinary life in the booming urban centres, where literacy was spreading and the vernacular language was gaining ground over the classical. The new Song literary culture also gave rise, in the religious sphere, to the appearance of anthologies of the words and deeds of a master, the *yulu* 語 錄 genre (recorded sayings), usually of Buddhist meditation or later, Neo-Confucian masters, but of Daoists as well. *Yulu* are not verbatim transcriptions but a restyling of reported speech, done into a kind of literary vernacular, all culled from an enormous pool of traditionally transmitted material, both oral and written. At the back of the *Yulu* genre are not only the apologetic and propagandist treatises in developed dialogue form popular from the 4th century on, but also elements of the ever popular miracle stories (*zhiguai xiaoshuo* 志 怪 小 說) contained in such works as 'On the Tracks of the Supernatural' (*Soushen Ji* 搜 伸 記) by Gan Bao 干 寶 (first half of 4th cent.), a collection of old folk legends showing traces of Indian borrowing[44] and still in vogue in the China of today. The *yulu* form also looks forward to the later full development of the *gong'an* 公 案 (Precedent Cases) genre, one of the most remarkable forms of the teaching story to come out of Buddhist China.

Song Emperor Zhenzong, 真 宗, who ascended the throne in 998, apart from his patronage of Buddhism, was also a keen Daoist. He is said to have had a visionary visitation from a Divine Being telling him that three sacred passages from 'The Auspicious Talismans of the Great Mean' (*Dazhong Xiangfu* 大中祥 符)) were about to descend. The Emperor promptly changed the reign title, after only four years, from *Jingde* 景 德 (Great Virtue) to *Dazhong Xiangfu* (1008-17).[45] In 1016 his reign published the third *Daozang* (Daoist Canon, also split into three 'grottoes' mirroring the Fozang – Buddhist Canon's three 'baskets'). In fact the increasingly complex interactions between Daoism, Buddhism and

---

[43] For an animated production of this extraordinary scroll-painting go to http://youtu.be/ MX14haeDebk

[44] For example, in the teaching of reincarnation CL: 180

[45] On the heavenly letters see Cahill, Suzanne E. 'Taoism at the Sung Court: The Heavenly Text Affair of 1008', *Bulletin of Sung and Yuan Studies* 16 (1980): 23-44.

the local folk religion practised by the village shamans (*wu* 巫) were gradually integrated into a bureaucratically controlled state pantheon.

Buddhism, by now a deeply rooted thousand year growth in Chinese soil, was thus consciously synthesised with Daoism and Confucianism. It was also to give rise to an unexpected philosophical ferment that came to a head in the school of Neo-Confucianism, a form of governance which was to prevail right into modern times. First, Zhou Dunyi 周 敦(1017-1073) took the term *Taiji* 太 極 (Supreme Ultimate) from the ancient Book of Changes (易經 *Yijing)* and schematised the relationships between *yin* 陰 and *yang* 陽 and the Five Elements 五 行, whilst the brothers Cheng Hao 程 顥 (1031-1085) and Cheng Yi 程 頤 (1032-1107) were largely responsible for establishing the Four Books – *Mencius* 孟 子, *The Great Learning* 大 學, The *Doctrine of the Mean* 中庸 and the *Analects* 論 語 of Confucius as the backbone of Chinese literary and political culture, and of its education system. The emphasis is ever on their applicability to the furtherance of social and political continuity: to governance. Yet as Arnold Toynbee says,

'The five Far Eastern philosophers, culminating in Zhuxi, who, in the course of the eleventh and twelfth centuries of the Christian Era, created a new system of metaphysics and ethics in the belief that they were rediscovering the original meaning of the Confucian Classics, owed less to the authentic Confucian canon than to a Mahāyanian *Weltanschauung* which by their day had so subtly permeated the intellectual atmosphere of the Far Eastern World that it could govern the thought of minds that were set upon ignoring or repudiating it.'[46]

In the second half of the tenth century the rule of law had stabilised, reflected in four great compilations evincing the critical literary spirit of the age, which came into being at this time. The *Taiping Guanji* 太平廣記, (Comprehensive Anecdotes from the Taiping Xingguo period, 976-984), a compendium of ghost stories and miracle tales (*zhiguai* 志怪 and *chuanqi* 傳奇) in 500 chapters compiled by Imperial decree as part of a vast general collection of literature of the

---

[46] Toynbee, Arnold, *A Study of History*, vol. V, p. 49. Oxford, 1954. Rprt., 1979. See also vol. IX, p, 40-45 for Toynbee's treatment of the Neo-Confucian renaissance: rather out of fashion now, Toynbee's views are still of interest today for their breadth and originality.

Song, was completed in 978. The printing of this work was cancelled but the woodblocks were kept. The work was ordered thematically and is a rich source for later vernacular literature.[47]

The *Taiping Yulan* 太平御覽, (The Imperial Overview of the Era of Great Peace, Preface dated 983) is a collection of literature in 1000 chapters, under 55 headings and three categories – Heaven, Earth and Man.

The *Wenyuan Yinghua*文苑英華 (The Literary Garden of Luxuriant Beauty), published in the 7th year of Taiping (982), is an anthology of poetry and anecdotes.

Cefu Yuangui 冊府元龜 , (The Archival Treasury of the Original Tortoise), i.e. the archival treasury of the spiritually endowed longevity of dynastic government (the tortoise being sacred to China and an emblem of longevity, strength and endurance), a chronological survey in 1000 chapters relating the historical deeds of the ruling class up to the 2nd year of the Jingde reign period (1006), with a preface written by Emperor Zhenzong himself (1013), was compiled by the influential literati Yang Yi 楊億, a high-ranking Hanlin academician and bureaucrat, together with his co-editors. It took eight years to compile this vast work.

---

[47] CL: 204

Prince of Literature (Gong Wen 公文)

Yang Yi, editor-in-chief of the *Cefu Yuangui*, was a key figure of the Northern Song dynasty and in the thick of literary developments at court at the beginning of the eleventh century. He was born in 974 in Pu Cheng 浦城, on the border of Zhejiang 浙江 and Fujian 福建. His father, before the boy's birth, had had a dream that a Daoist priest by the name of 'jade-embodying mountain man' (*Huaiyu Shanren* 懷玉山人) came to call on him. When the boy was born he was covered with hair over a foot long, which disappeared after a month. He did not speak for some years but one day, being carried to the top of a pagoda, burst out with the following famous lines:

> Upon this tall pagoda's peak
> My hands can almost embrace the stars
> I dare not raise my voice to speak
> For fear of startling the supreme repose.[48]

At the age of seven this child prodigy was already highly skilled in composition and able to converse on profound subjects, and when he was eleven Emperor Taizong 太宗 sent for him to Court. He later became a poet, scholar, influential politician, court intimate, dedicated Buddhist and Hanlin academician, employed, among other tasks, in preparing the dynastic annals, drafting Imperial Edicts and the arrangement of the Buddhist Tripiṭaka.[49] At the age of 30, when the Khitan-Liao tartars were raiding Shanzhou in Hubei and Emperor Zhenzong's forces were facing possible defeat, he was found drinking and dancing on the city wall with the commander of the campaign, his friend Kou Zhun (d.1023), who had persuaded the Emperor to come in his imperial person to oversee the confrontation.[50] The Emperor felt strangely encouraged by this sight and indeed, shortly afterwards Khitan leader General Xiao Talin

---

[48] Slightly adapted from Giles, CBD: 2387, who translated from the *Song Shi,* chap. 305, fasc. 64.

[49] Yang Yi gained the *Jinshi* 進士 degree (higher than the modern PhD) at the early age of eighteen.

[50] Kou Zhun was Prime-minister from 1004-1006 CE.

was picked off by an elite Song crossbow sniper, whereupon the enemy Liao 遼 sued for peace (which alas did not last[51]).

When Yang Yi's mother fell ill he had requested the Emperor to release him from official duties in order to look after her in the south. As there was no opportunity to consult the Emperor he left on his own initiative. The Emperor approved of his action by letter.[52] This is extraordinary treatment for a mere Imperial administrator. Indeed his presence at court seemed at times almost indispensable and the up-and-coming literati all relied on Yang Yi for appraisal for he was the one they had to pass on their way to a further career. Many in the capital were also jealous, slandering and vilifying him but the Emperor set great store by him.

When the Emperor Zhenzong wished to set the Empress Liu on the throne the court was against it but the Emperor wished Yang Yi to draft the edict. To this end the Emperor told the Prime Minister, Ding Wei,[53] to ask Yang Yi to draft it, but he was unwilling. Ding Wei said to Yang Yi, 'You are urged to do it; do not worry about riches and honour.' 'This kind of riches and honour is not what I seek,' replied Yang Yi. Then Ding Wei got another to write the edict and Yang Yi resigned on the grounds of ill health. Foreseeing an early death Yang Yi sought to escape this by giving himself the cognomen 'length of years' (*Da Nian*大年) but he died at the age of 47, in high favour as ever and back at his post.

A precocious Yang Yi, in the middle of the new literary culture spreading out from the centre, seemed to espouse the call of the day, 'spontaneity', in place of the traditional classical language. Actually his preferred literary orientation was for the erudite and classical, thus going completely against the prevailing taste. He was the central figure in a group of poets calling themselves the *Xikun Pai* 西崑派 'West Kun Group'[54] who sought to emulate the poetic style of the Tang poet Li Shangyin 李商隱 (812-858), whose poetry was extremely abstruse, sophisticated, multilayered and full of hidden satire. The Xikun group[55] laid great stress on harmony, refinement and accuracy of expres-

[51] Peers, J.C., *Soldiers of the Dragon: Chinese Armies 1500 BCE-1840 CE.* Oxford, 2006.
[52] Song Shi, 305.14
[53] See Giles :1942
[54] See Jin Qian, *Formation of the Xikun style Poetry,* Thesis submitted to the Univ. of Massachusetts, 2009.
[55] Xikun here refers to the West Kunlun Mountains, where the library of legendary Emperors was said to be located. See Jin Qian, op.cit. Introduction, p.1. That the Kun-

sion. Yang Yi liked playing poetry games: he and his friends started exchanging poems or trying to cap each other's verses[56] in the style of Li Shangyin, whilst working on the editing of the *Cefu Yuangui* (1005-1013). But in 1008 their activity stopped abruptly.[57] Still, the consequent 'Xikun' poetry style was the fashion at court for over forty years afterwards even though the Emperor was displeased with this erudite verse, thick with allusions that only the highly educated could follow. Someone had informed him that buried in all those allusions were masked criticisms of the Emperor himself. An Imperial edict was then issued forbidding the writing of ornate poetry, which put an end to the publication of Xikun poetry collections.[58] This was a very dangerous game

lun Mountains also constitute the celestial library where the definitive editions of the sacred books of the Daoists are kept, as well as being the home of The Queen Mother of the West, or, to give her Her proper title, 'The Ninefold Numinous Grand and Realised Primal Ruler of the Purple Tenuity from the White Jade Tortoise Terrace' (*zi wei yuan ling bai yu gui tai jiu ling tai zhen yuan jun*) – the title given her by Tao Hongjing and still used today (see Suzanne Cahill, *Transcendence and Divine Passion*. Stanford, 1993, pp. 33-36) – goes to show the interpenetration of Daoism and Buddhism in the spiritual life of the Confucian literati of the time, as well as the sense of temporal continuity still present in the Sinic world.

[56] There was a long tradition of capping another's verse in literati circles in China. See *Zen Sands* by Victor Sogen Hori, Intro. , p.44, on how this would influence later Chan training procedures.

[57] '…however, from the fourth year of the Jingde reign period (1007), Emperor Zhenzong dedicated himself to various Taoist religious activities including faking books from heaven and celebrating auspicious omens. In the fourth month of the first year of the *Dazhong xiangfu* 大中祥符 reign period (1008), he issued an edict that in the tenth month he would conduct the *feng* and *shan* sacrifices, which were sacrifices offered respectively on Mt. Tai to heaven and on Mt. Liangfu to the earth. The last poems in *Xikun ji* were written in the autumn of 1008. In other words, the poetry exchange stopped before the entire country entered the craze for auspicious omens and Taoist activities.' *Jin Qian*, p.110.

[58] The Edict *Jieyue zhuci fuyan ling yu diaoyin wenji zhuanyunshi xuan wenshi kanxiang zhao* 誡約属辭浮艶令欲雕印文集轉運使选文士看詳詔 [Commandment to Admonish and Restrain Pompous and Unsubstantial Literary Compositions and Ordering Literary Collections that Are to Be Printed with Blocks of Wood Be Examined by Men of Letters Chosen by an Official of Transportation], was issued to ban the new style in the first month of the second year of the Dazhong xiangfu reign period (1009), *Song Da Zhaoling ji, juan* 19, p.70. Quoted in Qian, p.111-112. This put a stop to the *xikun* poetry exchanges as the new Daoist rage came in to vogue at court.

that Yang Yi was playing, but interestingly enough he seems to have got away with it – even though some of these poems were obviously a little more than 'frivolous and decadent'. But there was a long tradition in China of the virtuous minister, of flawless moral and political integrity, (qualifications Yang and some of his friends in similar positions seemed to have possessed) criticising the Emperor.[59]

Being highly placed in court circles, Yang was naturally in touch with the religious currents of the day. He himself seems to have undergone a spiritual crisis that expressed itself in ill health, around 1005 and again in 1008, between the ages of 31 and 34. In a letter to his friend Li Wei 李維 (961-1031), thirteen years his senior, who also participated in the compilation of the *Cefu yuangui,* he relates years of being sunk in chronic disease brought about by a spiritual malaise due to his lack of direction amid all the fame and fortune of court life. Finally he finds his way to Mount Lu, to the Buddhist mountain monastery reestablished more than half a century earlier by the famous Chan Master Fayan Wenyi 法眼文益 (885-958). Listening to the talks in the monastery, 'the blockage of ignorance was suddenly released' and six months later 'vast and open there was no more doubt, it was like remembering something which had been forgotten'. Even Yang Yi the consummate poet could do no better than write of his Buddhist conversion that 'it was like suddenly awaking from sleep. All the tensions were peacefully at rest and suddenly the self fell off'.[60] From now on he had no more doubts and was later closely associated with the Linji Chan masters Guanghui Yuanlian (951-1036)[61] and Yuncong Cizhao of Gulin Shan (965-1032).[62]

---

[59] Yang Yi, in writing a certain *xuanqu* 宣曲 verse on the Han Emperor Wudi and his behavior towards his concubines, was thought to be criticising Emperor Zhenzong. His services were obviously too valuable to the Empire, which could not do without his gifts as an editor, writer and instrument for the popularisation of the Song cultural ethos.

[60] *Chanlin Sengbao Chuan,* 禪林僧寶傳 (A Treasury of Monks' Biographies from the Chan Forest, X.79. 1560.) Albert Welter has done a lot of the donkey work in searching out the references and elucidating the intricate history behind the arising of the Linji faction to prominence at the Song court. See *www.thezensite.com* for the necessary articles and various books by Albert Welter, Professor and Head, Department of East Asian Studies, University of Arizona.

[61] X.78. No 1553, juan 18, 511c6-512a.

[62] Biography in GDL., X.78. No.1553, juan 17.

It seems then that Yang Yi was born at a most auspicious time: the second and third Song emperors wanted to consolidate their rule by transferring their power base from the military (which had actually brought the first Emperor Taizu to power) to civil authority. To this end they actively promoted the man of letters as an instrument for stabilising the new Song dispensation. In 977 the second emperor Taizong (r.976-97) announced his intention of using civil service examination candidates as the means to bring about order.[63] In that year some 5,000 men took the departmental examinations, in 992 it was over 19,000.

The new rules for civil service examinations greatly increased the influx of literate civil servants. Yang Yi was to a large extent one of the architects of this new impulse. Later, fifteen years after his death, the TCDL (see below) was published in 1036 and the new Song dispensation was consolidated by imperial recognition of the Linji line of Chan Buddhism as the official version of Chan in the Song. The preface to this work was written by the son-in-law of the Emperor Renzong and gave expression to the official line on the Linji School.

The *historical* interest of the CDL then has to do with Imperial patronage of Chan Buddhism used as a tool by the new dynasty in the process of differentiating its message in order to consolidate its power. This imperial message might be paraphrased as 'a special dispensation different from forgoing dynasties'. It was also a *written* message – the tremendous growth of printing, a voracious reading public eager for participation in the new Song ethos and new forms of vernacular prose emerging all contributed to the literary revolution. The inchoate dialogue form of the CDL too asks for an on-going participation from the reader, who is involved in an in-depth appreciation of an evolving complexity, as much to do with the vicissitudes of time and place as with the opening up of a new way to liberation and the awareness of one's roots – all in one work.

---

[63] See Bol, Peter K., *This Culture of Ours: Intellectual Transitions in T'ang and Sung Culture*. Stanford University Press, 1992, p.54 and Chaffee, John W., *The Thorny Gates of Learning in Sung China*. Albany: State University of New York, 1995, p.49.

The Chan School of Buddhism

The word Chan, better known in its Japanese translation, 'Zen', is originally an Indian word (*dhyāna*) rendered into Chinese, meaning anything from 'meditation' to 'meditative absorption'. The Chan School's historical arising in China cannot be traced further back than the middle of the 7th century. With the Sixth Patriarch Huineng's 惠能 (638-713 CE) teaching of 'Sudden Awakening' a new orientation within the Buddhist community arose. Huineng's teaching later caused a schism within a part of the Chinese Sangha (community of monks), who were until then primarily devoted to harmonious co-existence. After Huineng a polarisation took place into a 'conservative' Northern Chan school, and the new 'sudden awakening' of southern Chan. The schism was the making of Southern Chan, the decline of the Northern.[64]

The many geographically separated regional monasteries in China had always been closely connected by the tradition of pilgrimage. Monks usually studied under various Masters and some seem to have been almost continuously on the road.[65] Yet each establishment also had its own 'house style'. These styles were not determined by a rigid adherence or membership to any school before Huineng, but by the quality and style of leadership of the master in residence. The initial schism caused by the Sixth Patriarch of Chan and the consequent fragmentation of a section of the Buddhist community also obliged those affected to give more definite expression to an inchoate identity, based on a more conscious affiliation. A proto-Chan family emerged and during the Song the different Chan house styles, through the literary efforts of politically powerful and gifted literati such as Yang Yi, were arranged under one family tree with various distinct branches.[66] This important development was a Song-created Chan, a newly identifiable school of Buddhism in China based, for legitimisation purposes, on the myth of a long patriarchal transmission. The

---

[64] Though this is probably wrong: Tangut Buddhism in the north-west had a thriving Buddhist culture. See Dunnell, Ruth W., *The Great State of White and High: Buddhism and State Formation in Eleventh-Century Xia*. Hawaii, 1996.

[65] Kraft, Kenneth, *Eloquent Zen: Daito and Early Japanese Zen*. Hawaii, 1992, p.34.

[66] For a detailed treatment of how the branches came to grow out as they did, see *The Mystique of Transmission* by Wendi Adamek. Harvard, 2007.

school was also to serve as a paradigm for the stability of dynastic transmission, through the literati who edited the texts in conformity with the prevailing *Zeitgeist*. A potent stimulus to the religious and cultural life of the Song dynasty and beyond was the result of these activities.

The first canonical work of the Chan School emerged during the Song dynasty. Despite, or because of, its sophisticated editing by Yang Yi *et al* the *Jingde Chuandeng Lu* 景德傳燈錄, (Records of the Transmission of the Lamp to the Jingde [reign period 1004], CDL) was published around 1008 and established and legitimised the acceptance of a religious movement whose exclusive attention, outside of the Chinese kinship system, was to the gaining of Buddhist liberation, even 'outside of the scriptures'. The conservative society in which this occurred, because it was geared primarily to its own perpetuation, learned to use this powerful movement within its body politic. There was an active political accommodation between government and the Chan School.[67]

The young man drinking and dancing on the city walls of Shanzhou, canonised on his death in 1020 as 'Prince of Literature', was responsible, more than any other man, for establishing the new orientation of the Chan School of Buddhism as a school apart from all others. Yang's editing of the CDL, compiled originally by an unknown monk named Dao Yuan 道原, is a hefty biographical compendium in thirty books, of 981 Chan masters' transmission stories and verses from all schools, with additional anecdotes of some 700 persons. Yang also wrote the preface. It is therefore the *locus classicus* for getting to know the larger family of those now officially recorded for the first time as being engaged on this Chan Way. Actually the work turned out to be a real *tour de force*, far outlasting the temporary concerns of *Realpolitik*, for it has been in continuous use as a source of Chan anecdotes, training stories and precedents (*gong'an* 公案) for the last thousand years. Defining the new Chan identity was the old idea of a family 'lineage', the central concern of the dynastic succession too. But the affiliations of the Chan family tree of the CDL would be through spiritual affinity rather than that of blood, the lineage traced retrospectively to an incommensurable *Urzeit* before the existence of any dynasty and would far outlast that institution into the future.

---

[67] There was a prolific mushrooming of State Chan monasteries during the early Northern Song period. See *How Zen Became Zen* by Morten Schlutter, Kuroda Studies in East Asian Buddhism 22. Hawaii University Press, 2008, pp.48-52

Chan Masters Fayan and Linji

The religious affiliation of Yang Yi the politician, at the time of working on the CDL was Chan Buddhist. He was initially a follower of the great Chan Master Fayan Wenyi 法眼文益 (885-958), founder of his own Chan 'school'[68] whose principal area of influence, Wuyue 吳越, was close to Yang's birthplace. The old kingdom in Zhejiang province was a prosperous state on the coast, manufacturing silk and ceramics. Its principal attraction for Buddhism since the pre-Song upheavals was the cultured atmosphere flourishing there, a veritable haven for Southern Buddhism.[69] But Master Fayan, despite his intellectual culture, fondness for paradox, broad knowledge rooted in the Buddhist and Chinese classics and his profound insight into the *Avatamsaka Sutra* (*Huayan Jing* 花嚴經 Flower Ornament Sutra), was always primarily devoted to helping disciples towards the sudden awakening of Huineng's school. He was also responsible for restoring Buddhist training centres on Tiantai and Lu mountains. He was no mere man of learning but had a gift for demonstrating the ordinariness of the transcendental.[70] All learning was grist to the mill of his great Heart. The lineage to which he gave birth not only produced the CDL but also the eclectic *Zongjing lu* 宗鏡錄 (Records from the Mirror of the Chan School[71]) by Yongming Yanshou 永明延壽 (904-975), one of the great names in Chinese Buddhist literature. Yanshou and Daoyuan, compiler of the CDL, were Dharma-brothers (they had the same teacher, Tiantai Deshao, 天台德韶 891-975 CE, an heir of Master Fayan). In the old kingdom of Wuyue they were still concerned with *preserving* the harmony and eclectic nature of all the Buddhist Schools rather than their simplification and popularisation, especially in a world recently torn apart by wars. Fayan had many Dharma-heirs and his influ-

---

[68] He appears in chapter 24 and again in chapter 28 of the CDL.

[69] Members of the royal family of the former Wuyue kingdom were also active in the social circles of the Xikun poets centring on Yang Yi. Jin Qian, op.cit. p.66.

[70] Following Dumoulin, Vol.1, pp.233-6.

[71] T. 48, no. 2016. I have translated it by this title in the belief that Yanshou was trying to *preserve* a mature, authentic Buddhist practice by encoding it in this masterpiece and unlike our author of the CDL, Daoyuan, was lucky enough to slip through Yang Yi's net! But for a different point of view on Yanshou see Albert Welter, *Yongming Yanshou's Conception of Chan in the Zongjing lu.* Oxford, 2011.

ence extended even to Korea, where his eclecticism was also much appreciated in a newly united country.

The earlier Chan master Linji Yixuan 臨濟義玄 (d.866), retrospective progenitor of another school of Chan,[72] was a master of singular originality in the directness and simplicity of his message. His devoted heirs, for five generations after his death, kept his teaching alive and served the Song renaissance well in its desire to promote a more 'spontaneous' literature with a broader appeal and function. Master Linji's teaching was distinctive for its liveliness and *concreteness*. In the *Huayan* philosophy to which Master Fayan leaned, the interpenetration of appearance and reality, of relative and absolute is strongly emphasised. The locus for this interpenetration in Linji's Chan is the human being in all his immediate physicality, with his innate capacity for pre-verbal understanding. The concrete *is* the transcendental. Enlightenment is immanent. The difference between the two masters was really only one of emphasis. The true human being according to Linji is a person of no fixed, permanent attributes. He is ultimately without characteristics, without root, without source. However much one might search for some identifiable permanent essence, it is not to be found. Ultimate reality is here and now, in this concrete existence. The human being is essentially empty by virtue having no self-nature, but he is not insentient. On the contrary, when he is truly himself he is no different from the Buddhas and Bodhisattvas because only then can he be said to be properly alive, free of any dysfunctions. Buddha is just the miraculous functioning of the everyday man in his daily activities, which is the endless life of the Buddhas and Patriarchs. This more immediate, down-to-earth teaching appealed to the spirit of the times.

The history of Linji and Fayan's legacy is complex. Linji's story exemplifies the problems faced by the modern investigator of Chan as an historical phenomenon.[73] He died in 866, was actually 'reborn' in 1036, when the *Tiansheng Guang Deng Lu* 天聖廣燈錄 (Extended Transmission of the Lamp

---

[72] In Japanese his name is Rinzai, whose school was to flourish mightily – and still is – in Japan and the wider world. He appears in chapters 12 and 28 of the CDL.

[73] See Welter, Albert, *Monks, Rulers and Literati: The Political Ascendancy of Chan Buddhism.* Oxford, 2006 and his other works, which offer an in-depth appreciation of the complexities of Chan history, as well as Halperin, Mark, *Out of the Cloister: Literati Perspectives on Buddhism in the Song.* Harvard, 2006, for a good treatment of the issues.

to the Tiansheng period, TCDL), the follow-up to the CDL, was published. This is another important biographical collection, compiled by no less a personage than Li Zunxu 李遵勖 (988-1038), brother-in-law of Emperor Renzong 仁宗 (r.1023-64), father Emperor Zhenzong (968-1022), a follower of the Linji School. The work is important for two principle reasons; firstly, that the phrase 'a special transmission outside the teachings', which seems so characteristic of Linji Chan, makes its first appearance here (Yang Yi had already set the stage in his preface to CDL by calling the school 'a special *practice* outside the teachings') and secondly because Master Linji himself also makes his first 'modern' appearance in this collection. This newly refashioned literary Record (*Lu*) of Linji and the 'perfected' version, in 1120, is the ahistorical and in a sense, the true one, destined to endure in terms of future influence. The CDL Linji is probably a little nearer to the rather quiet and reclusive original master, who died in the flesh in 866. The follow-up to the CDL (the TCDL) is an Imperial endorsement of the Linji school as a vehicle for propagating Song literary and spiritual culture. The accent in the TCDL is no longer on historical details but on teachings which afford an interesting glimpse into the development of the *yulu* itself.

The encounter dialogue style characteristic of the *yulu* form is also a product of the literary artistry of Song literati. The editors of the CDL must have been aware of being players on a stage, part of the forces of history. As a group of elite civil servants they were producing literature of the highest quality for specific political goals, in obedience to the *Zeitgeist* – and in the act transcending it. Put another way, even gifted Song dynasty literati did not have it in their power to create works for *purely* political or sectarian purposes. These works proved capable of outlasting the exigencies of a particular passing fashion or regime. The *Zeitgeist* had a broader and deeper compass and was pulling the strings.

The understanding of Yang and his team moves with the *Zeitgeist* though its sympathy was with the Fayan line, with cultured poetry and abstruse writing, which was challenged by the passing clouds of *Realpolitik*. These sympathies retreat into the background in favour of the 'Linji faction' masquerading as the vogue at court (it can only be known in retrospect that the passing vogue was the *Zeitgeist* in disguise). Yang, editor-in-chief, writes the preface, in which he tentatively starts the ball rolling with his 'a special *practice* outside the teachings'. Perhaps he even had an intimation that he and his band had created an enduring masterpiece, which would come to further fruition in the famous Chan phrase 'a special *transmission* outside the teachings' (1036) – the new Song cultural ethos had stabilised itself.

Apart from the fame of the *Xikun* movement, whose vogue lasted some forty years, Yang Yi also gets a sizeable biography in the official Song Dynastic History (chapter 305, fasc. 64) and a mention in the follow-up to the CDL, the TCDL[74] – he has not only been received into the Imperial bosom but also into the official pantheon of Chan immortals. He was, after all, a beloved bureaucrat and son, a literary prodigy posthumously canonised as 'Prince of Literature' (*Wen Gong*). His recasting of Daoyuan's work[75] established a new genre of literature that would endure for literally ages. That the *denglu* genre also had an influence outside of Buddhist literature can be gleaned from the Confucian masters of the southern Song; Zhu Xi's 朱熹 own *Yiluo Yuan Yuanlu* 伊洛淵源錄 (Records of the Origins of the Luoyang School), the *Ming Ruxue'an* 明儒學案 (Records of the Ming Scholars) by Huang Zongxi 黃宗羲 (1610-1695) of the Ming dynasty, the Qing dynasty's *Rulin Zongpai* 儒林宗派 (The Forest of Scholars from the Confucian School) by Wan Sitong 萬斯同 (1638-1702) are all modelled on the *denglu* genre.[76] In 1153, due to the many repetitions in the *denglu* works, a monk from the Linji school, Puji, 普濟 (1179-1253) deleted the redundancies and published 'The Five Lamps Meeting at the Source' 五燈會元,[77] a work in which the different schools were more clearly distinguished and the language simplified. The book gained a wide circulation even to the point of seeming to supplant the originals. Yet there were many things lacking in the 'Five Lamps', poetry and stories, which could only be found in the CDL and its follow-ups.

The future would see the Chan seed transplanted to Korea and Japan, to take root and flourish there. The importance of the CDL as a spiritual document was recognised from the very first in Japan. *Myōchō* 妙超 (better known as Daitō Kokushi 大燈國師 'the Great Lamp National Teacher' 1283-1337), the founder of *Daitōkuji* Monastery 大德寺 in Kyoto, made a copy of it in his own

---

[74] X. 78, 1553, 511c-12a.

[75] Daoyuan gets a mention of just eleven characters in the Song History, 'Monk Daoyuan, Jingde Records of the Lamp Transmission, 30 chapters.' 僧道原景德傳燈錄三十卷. See *Song Shi* 宋史, 205. 5186, 'the bibliographical sketches'.

[76] XY, Intro.

[77] X. 80. 1565.

hand in just forty days.[78] 'This is indeed the spiritual activity of a thousand sages, the life artery of the heroic patriarchs', he said.[79] Some seven hundred years of practice later and still going strong, Chan became, through the Japanese scholar Daisetz T. Suzuki, a movement known worldwide as 'Zen'. Even those with a limited interest in the Zen of our time are often familiar with Song dynasty Chan's great verse, the first mature proclamation of its message to the world, which appeared in 1108 and reads,

A special transmission outside the teachings
Not standing on the written word
Pointing directly to the human heart
See into its nature and become Buddha.[80]

---

[78] Kraft, op.cit. p.48.
[79] Kraft, op.cit. p. 163.
[80] X.64. 5. 377b & 379a dated 1108 CE.

Difficulties encountered by readers of the CDL

Only twenty-three years after the first publication of the CDL Grand Councillor Wangsui 王隨, an administrator of the highest rank and adherent of the Linji line, having realised that the vast complexity of the book was difficult even for the learned men of his own time to appreciate, published an influential edited-down version in one volume, of fifteen books and called it 傳燈玉英集 (The Collected Essence of the Transmission of the Lamp), 1034.

How much the more then might the modern Westerner, without any previous background knowledge, experience problems when confronted with such a work? The difficulties are compounded by the fundamental difference of outlook prevailing in the East and West. It was and still is proper in the East to adopt an outwardly reactive attitude (*wuwei* 無為) towards action, to lay the personal aside in order to become merged with the greater totality of what is going on. To find the Dao 道, the young monk's objective was to re-direct life energy towards losing the identity with personal desires and phobias. He left the home life to enter the religious life, there to direct the gaze inwards by rigorous meditation practice and outwards by strict observance of monastic codes of morality, a training considered sufficient to empty him of enough desires and phobias so as to make room for a clearer vision of the ground of his being, which normally lies hidden within. No longer in a state of servitude to the world and its inducements, there was little opportunity to chase after desires, for that would be to misdirect precious life forces to merely wrestling with endless temptations, whose satisfaction would bring no permanent happiness.

With Western man on the other hand, the personality occupies a central place in life and is attended by the assumption of a progressive development in the course of the satisfaction of desires. Everything is seen in relation to 'I'. The 'I' gives rise to desires, impulses and passions, with two consequences: first, one is able to became a progressively free and independent being to some extent, by virtue of being able to choose to re-act to being fired up by enthusiasms for what one thinks, feels and wills, or *not* to react. On the other hand, being usually carried away by these very desires, the victim becomes an easy prey to harmful forces through the over-indulgence of unhealthy passions, emotions and fears that bring no lasting peace.

These two approaches, the Eastern and the Western, although becoming less differentiated, are still present and have to be born in mind when reading such texts as the CDL, which is after all a complex product of Indo-Chinese-Buddho-Daoist-Confucian spiritual and literary culture with a thousand-year long maturation behind it. There are therefore some common pitfalls to be met in reading the literature of Chinese Chan and Far Eastern Zen. The well-travelled Chan way is still unfamiliar to us. Reductionism, the primary pitfall (the 'it is nothing but...' syndrome), is often the first recourse in the absence of understanding. That we should not be so sure of our own judgements seems obvious enough, considering that basic insights taken for granted in the Far Eastern religions are strange to the West. Modern interpreters of these insights, being often wholly unfamiliar with their contents as *practical* wisdom, attempt a rational explanation based on inexperience and lack of understanding.

It is often doubly confusing therefore to be also confronted with a simplistic handling of insights gained by an occidental 'interpretation'. Spiritual practices perfected over millennia in Asia are almost invariably twisted into a Western intellectual tradition that has evolved on completely different lines of development, and which has only recently caught up, or so it thinks, with oriental ways of seeing things. This Western line of intellectual 'scientific' development, wonderful as it is, came to its present splendour by objectively excluding the very approach so familiar to an Eastern one, namely, subjectivity. Quantum and Relativity Theories have only just emerged in the West and are still considered an exotic interpretation of life's inner workings.

That the West has, since the work of Sigmund Freud, become increasingly interested in the subconscious workings of the human psyche inevitably brings the East ever closer to us. Yet the impact of such a momentous *psychic* event is by no means confined to rational processes: it needs a courageous leap into the source of thought itself. Where does the need for such a leap come from, how does it arise and what to do with it when it reaches the light of common day? We do not even know concretely where a thought comes from, nor appreciate the wonder of an average human attention span measuring full six seconds and which has taken aeons to consolidate. Our path ahead is therefore unimaginable. Certainly it will be a path both linear and circular, like walking in a straight line and ending at the beginning. A circle traversed without having to walk upside down!

So how did Daoyuan, or Yang Yi and his team manage to square the circle by giving shape to such an enduring literary monument as the CDL? The key figure, Yang Yi, had prodigious literary talents and was familiar with the mountain of literature on history and poetry through the ages. The Chinese language too, despite grammatical affinities with Western subject-verb-object languages, still manages to be slippery enough to baffle the intellect. The *Cuifu Gui*, for example, edited by a team of Hanlin scholars with Yang Yi at their head, contains 94 million characters, which in an English translation would fill approximately 2000 volumes and is a literary collection of the exploits of the ruling clans. What makes these stories so complex and difficult to follow rationally is that they often use the language of inference. Confucius had already said that, '[turn up] one corner, infer [the other] three' and this is the salient feature of much of Chinese literature. Subjects are often omitted after the first mention and the text is so loosely punctuated that it flows in a continuous and essentially holistic, circular stream notoriously difficult for the rational mind.

Yang Yi was also a practitioner of Chan and closely connected with three of the most accomplished Chan masters of his day. His society too had been steeped in Buddhism for over a thousand years. The many abstruse stories and insights contained in the CDL, although forming only a fraction of the oral tradition (as shown by the subsequent publication of four more collections of 'Lamp' chronicles, albeit with duplications), all passed under Yang Yi's critical eye and editorial experience. The canonical work that emerged, the very first Chan 'Lamp' history, was the result of merging wisdom, insight and political expediency for the purpose of giving shape to an inchoate Chan literary tradition that could serve the dynasty.

One of the pitfalls in the misreading of Chan texts in translation concerns the key term *xin* 心 – almost invariably translated in English as 'mind'. The primary Chinese meaning of *xin* however is 'Heart' – even the shape of the character is clearly recognisable as one (Chinese etymology); but the traditional Chinese meaning includes heart in the sense of the moral nature, the affections, as well the capacity for intelligent and wise judgement, for it has the same connotations as it has in many other cultures. *Xin* is thus the seat of wisdom born of experience; it is the organ of *appreciation.* The capacity for an in-depth appreciation matured by experience is traditionally attributed, rightly or wrongly, to this organ. The problem is that there is no suitable, single word in the English language – except 'Heart' (with a capital to include the above definition) in its broad, traditional sense – for what *xin* embraces. The most common kind of reductionism translates it as 'mind', sometimes implicitly as '*my* mind' or even worse, mind is taken as the brain! Yet this human heart of ours has an electrical charge *sixty* times greater than that of the brain.

46

The heart has of course been recognised as 'intelligent' by the traditions of many cultures. Even the physical heart recapitulates human evolution from the fish to *homo sapiens*, beginning its life in the womb as a tube, exactly like the heart of a fish. Later it develops two chambers, then three and finally four, thereby going through the entire recapitulation. Although the central power-house of the whole organism, the workings of the heart is little understood; in occidental scientific terms it is just a pump, but also a muscle. Yet if all the composted experience in the evolution of *homo sapiens* is inscribed there, and if this history of actions and reactions is encoded in genetic material spread throughout the cells of the living body, whose roads all lead back to this ancient citadel, then all this has proved impossible to decode until now. Thus there is no *direct* road to this ageless intelligence concentrated in, or signified by, Heart. Happily this leaves it free to function undisturbed by an interfering busy-body – *me* – who reduces it all to 'my mind' and further down still to brain. For this seemingly autonomous Sun and sum of everything may or may not be part of a material continuum-individuality, may or may not be a separate awareness whose presence is unknown to the aggregation of sense organs making up the daytime feeling of 'I', yet its character – traditionally – is the colour of my actions and reactions, together with 'my' physical make-up, talents, shortcom-ings and 'my' propensities for this or that. It is my very body chemistry, which is attractive to some and repellent to others.

The *mind* as such is the sixth sense according to Buddhism. One of the darkest and most confusing areas is the still virtually uncharted region called simply Mind. We are justified in saying 'my' mind only to the extent that this 'my' happens to be in 'my' head, where I think and feel my mind to be localised and because the head is sitting on 'my' shoulders rather than on my neigh-bour's. However, to be able to call something truly mine usually means that it is at my disposal or under my control and power in some way, which is manifestly not the case when it comes to 'my mind', which I can neither turn on, nor off, at will. Well, if it isn't 'my' mind then whose is it?

Buddhist Mind as 'coherent cognition' might best be likened to a flat, calm expanse of water. With or without an object to reflect, one of the capacities of a sheet of water is to function as a reflector. In the absence of anything to reflect, the true, original and constant state of the calm surface of water would be a pristine purity capable of reflecting, with unerring accuracy, what falls into its compass. The perfectly flat, silver reflecting *surface* of water is also extraordinarily responsive to the slightest excitation from the environment, as well as having a calm, living depth of its own. It is an analogy for an aggregate awareness that functions in this reflective way. This mind, as the sixth sense, a reflector, is an aggregate of the other five senses, yet seems itself to have a double function. On the one hand it is an empty mirror-like awareness in sentient beings, therefore capable of receiving (reflecting) the impact of the perceptions of the other five senses and ordering their data, the more accurately the more it is purified of personal biases (the 'waves' of random thinking), and on the other hand has the capacity of experiencing *itself*, even when 'empty', or not receiving any data. It can be said to be the sixth sense because it occupies the middle ground by virtue of co-ordinating the other senses, just as the surface of a calm lake coordinates and reflects passing images.

That the Mind is capable of experiencing itself as empty or full, troubled or calm, is due however, to *xin*, Heart, which can be likened to the calm, living depths, the protean diversity, of deep water underneath the surface. This Heart is therefore unfathomable. In many traditions the hunch, passing instinct or intuition surfacing from the depths of this Oceanic Heart, is not considered a brain-based event. It surfaces rather, into the mind, which co-ordinates and pictures it by using images from the everyday world, giving form to the hunch, a seemingly urgent effort of the Heart to catch the attention of its host organism. The Heart's digestion processes (processing experience into wisdom) are responsible for sending up such impulses to the surface-mind and are often experienced as important cosmic burps by the host. Projected into the mind even in sleep, this receiver, the mind, can reflect and give form to data coming from both directions, from outside and from inside or underneath. Are these burps surfacing from the depths trying to say something then? Well, it might seem impossible to commune directly with this Ocean-Heart, but the repeated imagery it gives rise to seems to conform to a certain vocabulary, grammatical structure and mood.

How is it possible to develop a direct relationship with a Heart whose sheer physical dominance is expressed by an electrical charge sixty times greater than that of the brain? The study of the 'grammar' appearing in the mind, though an interesting subject in itself, is proverbially tricky. Any attempt on the part of the host to come into relationship with the sixth sense the mind, even more with the dark depths of the Heart underneath it, is therefore bound to be clumsy and insufficient if undertaken without backup support. Fortunately the approach to such an undertaking has been a science in India and China for quite a few thousand years already and is always ruled by a proper feeling of caution and humility, if not downright awe and reverence. It has been discovered that this Heart and its surface mirror Mind is actually friendly in a unique way, faithful and true. It is friendly because the vocabulary of the imagery thrown up is *individual* and true because the grammar is *universal*.

Normally however, there is not an inkling of the shocking extent of the autonomic nature of one's own Heart, itself miraculous. Is it surprising therefore that the host, 'me', has no means of interpreting the grammar of the imagery surfacing in the mind, never mind the seeming absence of mind?[81] These workings constitute a living activity of the interior environment.[82]

---

[81] 'A salt doll went to measure the depth of the ocean, but before it had gone far into the ocean it melted away. It became entirely one with the water of the ocean. Then who was to come back and tell of the ocean's depth?' Sri Ramakrishna. Also quoted by Jeffrey Moussaieff Masson in *The Oceanic Feeling: Origins of Religious Sentiment in Ancient India*. Reidel, 1980, p. 39.

[82] The above discussion on the heart is most curiously strengthened by just one example (there are many more) from our own culture, namely, the English translations of the works of the German philosopher Georg Fredrick Hegel (1770-1831). The translations of the works of Hegel into English afford the reader almost no access to Hegel's insights. The implications of this are enormous. The Western philosopher in many respects quite close to the spirit of the Eastern and Chinese teachings (see, for example, Needham, *Science and Civilisation,* vol.2, pp, 201, 291, 303, 466, 478; Fung Yu-lan, *A History of Chinese Philosophy,* vol. I, p.185; vol. II, p. 212) who yet attempted to bring a Western scientific rigour to bear on his own insights, has not been understood. A small example: to translate Hegel's term *Geist* by 'mind', (where 'Heart' or even 'spirit' might be more appropriate) often misses the point entirely and brings the same kind of problems as translating Chinese *xin* 心 by the same meaningless term. It is hardly surprising then that the insights themselves have yet to be understood.

49

The Gong'an

This leads us to the last difficulty, or in Chan 禪 terminology, the last gate (or 'portal' –*men* 門) encountered on the journey towards a fuller appreciation of such Chan texts as the CDL, namely, tackling the understanding of the *gong'an* 公 案 ('Precedent [teaching] Cases', in Japanese *kōan*). 'The most important characteristic of Sung Ch'an is the development of the Kung-an tradition'.[83] As a form of literature it is today irreducible to its parts and its uses in early times are difficult to trace.[84] The nearer it approaches the horizon of its own transcendence as mere anecdote, the more impossible it becomes to follow in- tellectually – the process seems suddenly to flip over into another dimension, like breaking through a barrier. Perhaps it was the Chinese genius for poetry together with its love of miracle stories of all kinds, coupled to an innate practi- cal cast of mind, which caused the slow growth of what came to be a Chinese Buddhist science of nurturing practical wisdom. It is wholly consistent with the spirit of the CDL, a work of literature espousing the practical teaching of 'not standing on the written word', that it should be the matrix for one of the most remarkable genres of literature in the world, the *gong'an*.

To a Song dynasty educated Chinese the literary form and content of what to modern readers seems so exotic and mysterious – the *gong'an* – would be a quite natural form of expression, given their cultural background. The Chinese language has the added advantage in that its characters are powerful visual images with an ancient history behind them. The character is not so much a picture – an image of a definite thing – as a web of allusions, cognate affini- ties and extensions of meaning that are unimaginable in an alphabetic system. Underneath the alphabetic system, which after all is a miracle of conciseness and *consciousness* in itself, lies that which brought it forth, namely, the crea- tive impulses residing in the human unconscious, rich in symbols and multiple

---

[83] Ishii Shûdô, 'Kung-an Ch'an and the Tsung-men t'ung-yao chi' in *The Kôan. Texts and Contexts in Zen Buddhism,* edited by Steven Heine and Dale S. Wright. Oxford Univer- sity Press, 2000, p.132 – a remark which firmly reinstates the Song Dynasty as one of the most important eras of Chinese Chan. 'Kong An' is the Wade-Giles transcription for Pinyin 'Gong'an'.

[84] Kraft, op.cit., p. 58.

meanings, the very source from which Chinese characters also spring. So there has never been any separation between intuition and rationality, even though certain trends developed individually – alphabets and characters. The Chinese are becoming increasingly aware of the virtues of an alphabetic system for the purposes of teaching literacy as the West is perennially interested in 'picture languages' as a means of undoing the stranglehold of the intellect.

It is impossible to discuss the history of Chan without mentioning the *gong'an* – perhaps one of the most extraordinary descents into the roots of language ever undertaken anywhere. A *gong'an* is a record of an encounter between a disciple who poses a question connected to his perennial quest and the master who responds in a whole-hearted way according to the needs of the disciple at that moment. The inner tension that prompts the disciple to question, encounters the skill, insight and long experience of the master who is responding. This encounter then creates a kind of explosion of meaning or insight in the student, the depth of which is commensurate with the tension within the disciple. Yet the disciple might or might not get the thrust of the master's hint, might or might not discern the volatile, dynamic mix of the push (which can even be physical on the contextual level) but the *record* of the encounter nevertheless always contains an entry point into a deeper level of reality, valid beyond the time and place which gave rise to the situation. These encounters later became precedents which were collected over time and formed part of a burgeoning corpus of Chan lore.

The utterances of the Buddha to his monks on how to deal with the day-to-day problems of living in a community dedicated to a re-linkage with the Buddha-nature in full awareness were later enshrined in the *Vinaya* texts. These became precedents to help future generations of practitioners. Similarly, the encounter dialogues which the early Chan masters had with their disciples and students were recorded – much later, and no doubt after much revision or outright invention (yet always functioning as a 'gateless gate' into another level of meaning). Taken from the common pool of a rich oral tradition and written materials circulating freely, they became precedents for later students: the *gong'an* were born. These encounter dialogues did not appear in print before the Song dynasty but their provenance as a genre could be very old and have their roots in many traditional forms of Chinese literary pastimes, ranging from stories of the miraculous to poetry competitions and the tradition of composing spontaneous capping phrases in group poetry meetings going back to well before the common era.

A classic example of a *gong'an* is when the Sixth Chinese Patriarch of Chan, Huineng, being told by the Fifth Patriarch to leave the monastery after receiving the transmission from him in the middle of the night, secretly departs into the dark. He is pursued the next day by a band of monks led by Daoming **(4.60)**, whilst the other monks fall behind on their way up the mountain in pursuit. It was presumed that Huineng had unlawfully absconded with the robe and bowl as tokens of the transmission from the Fifth Patriarch. Huineng, finally cornered by Daoming, is accused of stealing the robe and bowl. Huineng calmly lays both down on top of a rock and invites the monk to take them. When Daoming tries to pick them up they are so heavy he cannot lift them. Immediately appreciating the import of the awesome moment, he bows to Huineng and begs him not for the robe and bowl but for the True Dharma. At this crucial moment, Huineng utters the following words, 'Thinking neither of good nor of bad, at this very moment, what is your Original Face?' On hearing these living words Daoming at once awakens to a depth of insight different from the one he had been living in for so many years in the monastery of the Fifth Patriarch. He bows in gratitude, departs and later becomes a master in his own right. It is not therefore a matter of philosophy since the immediate physical reality is always a vital element in the encounter. [85] The master taking part in the encounter is qualified to respond because the 'Great Function' (*da yong* 大用) within him is activated and works without any obstructions (we are now in the very heart of Chan). What is the 'Great Function'? The Venerable Baoying **(12.303)** says, 'Everywhere they only have the *eye* for simultaneously breaking in and breaking out but they do not have the *function* of simultaneously breaking in and breaking out,'; so spiritual birth is likened to the birth of a chick from its egg – mother hen pecks from the outside at exactly the same time as the chick pecks from within and then there is birth. This is the great functioning at work.

The *Original Face* incident is recorded in the famous *Wumen Guan* (The Gateless Gate), a collection of forty-eight *gong'an* that first appeared in 1229 CE. (The first collection of *gong'an* was made by Fenyang Shanzhao, Jap. *Funyō Zenshō* 926-993 CE). Perhaps the greatest of the *gong'an* collections and a pearl of world literature is the *Biyan Lu* (Records from the Emerald Cliff, a.k.a. The Blue Cliff Records), a collection of one hundred *gong'an* put together by various contributors during the Song dynasty. Such collections are still in active use today as a means of deepening Chan practitioners' insight.

---

[85] For a good modern discussion of the *kōan* see ZS, introduction, pp. 3-90.

Verbal explanations then are of no use in working with *gong'an* – the first lesson of Chan – so how is the resolution to the challenge of '...what is your Original Face?' resolved? The *process* to meet that challenge is the business of every Chan practitioner, master or disciple and this process both is, and is not, unique. The Chan *gong'an* practice is unique in that it radically deconstructs iconographic, paradigmatic or imitative behaviour of any kind to reveal an inborn authentic naturalness slumbering in every human being, called by Channists 'The Buddha-nature'. Not unique are Chan's soteriological concerns, which are firmly rooted in mainstream Buddhist teachings that always lay the stress on practical experience – insight – rather than playing with empty abstractions.

If awakening is the business of the Buddhists then verification and authentication by a *bona fide* master as a means to preserve the integrity of the lineage came to be the ultimate expression of that in the Chan School. Someone who has been through the Chan training process and received authentication can easily probe the student, on any level, with a few questions (as seen time and again in the CDL) – and can therefore pass the teaching on. Yet the transmission from one master to another, for which the *lamp* is a metaphor, developed as a natural progression only after the Buddha's death. In the *Mahā Parinibbāna Suttanta* the Buddha, about to die, enjoins the assembly by saying to Ānanda, 'Therefore, O Ānanda, be ye a lamp unto yourselves. Be ye a refuge unto yourselves. Betake yourselves to no external refuge. Hold fast to the Truth as a lamp...'[86] The Chan School certainly came to follow these injunctions in principle through the realisation that one could only awaken to oneself and that that is different from being learned in the scriptures or being dependant on words. However, the Sangha, the community of those practicing the Buddha's Way, was already a stable institution during the Buddha's own lifetime and therefore provided a conducive environment to develop a practice whose every aspect would be distilled to its concrete essentials in China.

---

[86] *Dīgha Nikāya*.

The basic structure of
'The Records of the Transmission of the Lamp'

The entry to the CDL is through Yang Yi's preface. As to be expected from a literatus of such calibre, it is quite impressive in itself – not the prose of cold technical virtuosity but a sincere statement of editorial policy. According to this preface, the revision of Daoyuan's book turned on three principles. Firstly, that the truth had to be expressed in good literature, which is itself enriched by the sense of order and clarity which is able to differentiate the meaning in a clear and concise way; secondly, to get the historical order correct by verifying, as far as records allowed, the facts pertaining to senior Confucian officials and others traceable by virtue of their achievements, providing a reliable historical framework to the work as a whole and thereby revising the rather loose histories of previous times; and thirdly, to allow the Patriarchs to speak for themselves yet without repeating material on their lives already contained in the biographies of monks. It is the striving after the realisation of these principles that accounts for the high value of the CDL amongst the Chinese, Koreans and Japanese.

There is an interesting legend regarding the compiler of the CDL, Daoyuan. In a postscript dated 1132, to the second chapter of the *Zhongwu Jiwen* 中吳紀聞 by Gong Mingzhi 龔明之 (1091-1182) (Collected Stories from the Zhong and Wu Regions) a certain Zheng Ang 鄭昂 (n.d.) says that the CDL was compiled by an unknown Gong Chen 拱辰 (n.d.) at the Guanyin monastery 觀音 in Huzhou 湖州 and that whilst taking the book to the Capital, he showed it to a fellow monk travelling on the same boat en route for the Court. One night the book disappeared. Having reached the capital, this monk – Daoyuan 道原 – had already presented it to the court and the authorship was granted to him.[87] However, continues Zheng Ang, this story bears a remarkable resemblance to that told of the famous Jin scholar Guoxiang 郭象 plagiarising from Xiangxi

---

[87] See Wittern, Christian, *Das 'Yulu' des Chan-Buddhismus: Die Entwicklung vom 8.-11. Jahrhundert am Beispiel des 28. Kapitels des Jingde chuandenglu (1004)*. Peter Lang, 1998, p. 93, n.36.

向秀 his commentary of the Zhuangzi 莊子.[88] Anyway, Gong Chen's reported reaction to the theft by Daoyuan was to comment that his intention was merely to clarify the Way of the Buddhist Patriarchs and no more. Having achieved this, what was it to him whether the fame went to another? This remark was considered superb, with not a trace of revenge in the heart of Gong Chen.[89]

Chapters 1 & 2 of the CDL treat of seven Buddhas and twenty-eight Indian Patriarchs. The biographies of the Seven Buddhas opening the CDL proper go back to Twelve Buddhas, who go back to Twenty-four Buddhas, who go back to the Thousand Buddhas of every *kalpa*,[90] who go back and yet further back without end into the beginningless Continuum containing innumerable Buddhas embracing past, present and future.[91] In fact, Buddhas are everywhere because every atom contains uncountable 'Buddha-worlds'.[92]

From the very beginning of Buddhism in India the *Jātaka Tales* (former lives of the future Buddha), *Avadāna* (tales of the feats of the Bhodhisattva and great holy ones of Buddhism) and *Vyākarana* (explanations about the future) were an important vehicle for conveying moral teachings.[93] Early Buddhism might have got the idea of the Seven Buddhas from the Seven Rishis of the Rg-veda, but the immediate source is the *Mahāpadāna Suttanta* (the Sublime Story).[94] The transmission verses attributed to the Seven Buddhas and the twenty-eight Patriarchs had already appeared in the proto-Chan work *Baolin*

---

[88] CBD: nos. 1062 & 693.

[89] Paraphrased from the CDL, T.51. no.2076, 465b12-c1.

[90] There is a list of the Three thousand Buddhas, in the last, present and future *kalpa* in T. 14, nos. 446-8.

[91] The present aeon, called the *Bhadrakalpa* (the Good Aeon) will have a thousand Buddhas too, of which Buddha Shakyamuni was the fourth. The next Buddha will be Maitreya, after which come another 995, the last of whom will be named Roca. See further and the complete list, following Lamotte's *The Teachings of Vimalakirti* (translated into English by Sara Boin. Pali Text Society, 1976) p. 266, n.29, is to be found in F. Weller, *Tausend Buddhanamen des Bhadrakalpa nach einer fünfsprachigen Polyglotte.* Leipzig, 1928.

[92] The greatest *sutra* expounding this insight is the *Avatamsaka Sutra,* in Chinese *Huayan Jing,* T. 279, in English, *The Flower Ornament Scripture,* translated by Thomas Cleary. Shambhala, 1984.

[93] HIB: 683, p.757.

[94] *Dīgha Nikāya*, D. ii, 2, ff.

Zhuan 寶林傳 of 801 CE [95] and in the *Zutang Ji* 祖堂記 of 952.[96] In the CDL the Seven Buddhas are introduced as beings who have responded to the world for an immeasurable length of time without break and that each sat under a tree and there attained perfect awakening.

The first Tathāgata mentioned is Vipashin Buddha, the 998th of the previous *kalpa*, who lived in a time when the human life span was 80,000 years.[97] His transmission verse reads:

> The body undergoes birth from the midst of no-form
> Like a mirage emerging from various shapes;
> The heart of a mirage-man knows that originally there is nothing,
> Bad fortune or good, both are empty, for there is no resting place.

One of the key terms in Chinese Buddhism, inherited from the Sanskrit word *śūnyatā*, is *kong* 空, usually translated as 'emptiness'. But 'emptiness' means not very much to an occidental reader quite empty of the notions and vocabulary of oriental religion and philosophy. Even to gloss 'empty' as signifying, in Indian and Chinese Buddhism, the absence of any nuclear, independent and permanent essence in living-beings is difficult to understand. 'Emptiness'

---

[95] 'Transmission of the Baolin [Temple]' by Zhiju in *Zhongguo fojiao congshu: Chanzong bian* (Compendium of Chinese Buddhism: Chan School), 1.18:507-659. Reprint, Beijing: Jiangsu guji, 1993.

[96] 'Records from the Patriarchal Hall', Koreana Tripiṭaka no. 1503. The *Zutang Ji* contains early collections of documents from the oral tradition, passed down from the Five Dynasties and Tang times. It is of high research value for modern Chinese linguistics providing (if genuinely Chinese) important data indispensable for the study of the history of the modern Chinese language and an important source for research on Chan history.

[97] The *Drosophila* fruit fly, which helped to decode the mysteries of human D.N.A. and is still helping with research into human diseases, has an average life expectancy of ten days. It all depends which scale is being used. Such descriptions occur in our culture too: 'God had given Adam so huge a frame that when he lay down it stretched from one end of the earth to the other; and when he stood up, his head was level with the Divine Throne'. Quoted from Baba Bathra, 58a, a Tractate of the Babylonian Talmud in *Hebrew Myths: The Book of Genesis* by Robert Graves and Raphael Patai. Greenwich House, 1983. pp. 61-2. In the fourth *Deva Loka*, the *Tushita Heaven,* where all future Buddhas are said to be reborn before descending to earth, the normal life span is 4,000 [Tushita] years, which is 584 million earth years. (DCBT:343b)

might be better understood as total *relatedness;* there is no centre, therefore no essence and, unlike 'infinity', there is no abstraction. The Buddhas point the Way into the endless, the trackless, where nothing can be mapped, that is, absolutely known, where everything is open, naked and revealed as being just as it is, where the only truly human attribute that can flourish is awe, wonder and *appreciation.*

The transmission verses of the Seven Buddhas set the tone for what is to come. Even *karma* (good fortune or bad) is a mirage. A mirage has no root, no real or permanent nature. The Heart is originally birthless, since it comes into being moment to moment due to circumstances – take the circumstances away, then there is no heart. Buddha is one who realises this relatedness (emptiness) of all things, that there is no birth and death, only changes of state. Therefore there is no fear. All sentient beings, originally pure and free, having once come to experience the body and heart as empty, are freed from the suffering of birth and death, for all transformations are by nature impermanent.

The lion's roar of Buddha Shakyamuni, on being born, was to take seven steps to each of the four directions and with one hand pointing to heaven, the other to earth, emit the great roar, 'Above and below and in all directions I alone am worthy of reverence'. Later, at the appearance of the morning star early on the eighth day of the twelfth month the ascetic Gotama became Shakyamuni Buddha, the teacher of gods and men. After showing the Way for forty-nine years he said to his principal disciple, Mahākāśyapā, 'I now hand over to you the pure Dharma Eye of Nirvāṇa, the miraculous heart, the true form-without-form, the delicate and wondrous True Dharma. You should guard it and uphold it.'

It was Mahākāśyapā, the first Indian Patriarch and progenitor of Chan, who then requested Ānanda, whom the Buddha had praised as first in intelligence, to recollect the teachings (he had heard much and retained it all, like water poured from one vessel into another without a single drop being spilled). Ānanda, always obedient, prostrated himself before the assembly, ascended the Dharma-seat and spoke these undying words, 'Thus have I heard. At one time the Buddha was abiding in such and such a place and delivered such and such a teaching…' and so the corpus of Buddhist *sutras* was born. When it came to the time of his demise, Ānanda composed his own transmission verse.

Sanakavāsa, the recipient of this transmission, who became the third Indian Patriarch, went into the forest, as had been ordained, (he was not lost in the forest) to subdue two fiery dragons. Having tamed them, the very same ground became a Buddhist precinct, from which he gave forth the True Dharma.

The famous story of Upagupta, the Fourth Indian Patriarch who converted Mara, the Buddhist 'Evil One'[98], also appears in the 29th Vadāna (*Aśokāvadāna*[99]) of the *Divyāvadāna*, (Divine Tales)[100], a compendium of Indian Buddhist narrative tales, many extracted from the *Mūlasarvāstivādin Vinaya*, from the beginning of our era. There was a long tradition on mainland India, of the 'Masters of the Law' contained in the *Aśokāvadāna*[101] concerning the first five generations of Dharma heirs.

The last of the twenty-eight Indian Patriarchs is also the first Chinese Patriarch. Bodhidharma, progenitor of Chinese Chan, who came to China 'floating on the ocean deep where summer gave way to winter three times' and arrived in Nanhai, 南海 on the Pearl River Delta in Southern China, on the 21st day of the 9th month in the year 527 CE (These dates are not yet based on historical fact). Bodhidharma is the figurehead of the Chan School and throughout the CDL the standard question asked by many monks is, 'What is the meaning of the Patriarch's coming from the West?' – meaning, 'What is the meaning of Buddhism [coming to China]' or, stated philosophically, 'What is the purpose of Buddhism?' – this question is often abbreviated in the text to 'What is the meaning of the coming [from the West]?'

Books 3, 4 & 5, treat of the Chinese patriarchs, from First Patriarch Bodhidharma to the Sixth Patriarch Huineng. The Chan family resorts to the lamp as a metaphor for its transmission of the Dharma from master to master, likened to a torch lighting in relay the next one, so that the light may endure without a break.[102] The Sixth Patriarch, founder of the tradition of 'sudden awakening' which came to be known as the Southern School, underscores its message and gets it down to three words – 'Heart is Buddha'. The school of Bodhidharma

---

[98] Called 'Mara' in Buddhism, also 'Papiyan' "more wicked" comparative Sanskrit form of Papin, wicked. See *History of the Devil* by Paul Carus, 1900, Dover reprint

[99] In John Strong, *The Legend of King Aśoka: a study and translation of the Aśokavadāna.* Princeton Library of Asian Studies, 2002, pp. 173-197.

[100] Part I has been translated but the *Aśokavadāna* belongs to a future volume. *Divine Tales: Divyadāna Part I* translated by Andy Rotman, Classics in Indian Buddhism, Wisdom, 2008.

[101] T.2042, ch.2-3; T.2043, ch.6-9, following Lamotte. For the five Masters of the Law see Lamotte, HIB: .206-212 & p. 695ff.

[102] For a comparatively recent use of the lamp as a metaphor of transmission, see section 20 of the *Platform Sutra of the Sixth Patriarch,* trsl. Philip Yampolsky. Columbia University Press, 1967.

comes to a head with the master Huineng 惠能 **(5.71)**, from whom two broad lineages are discernible, the one emanating from his heir Qingyuan Xingsi 青原行思 **(5.83)**, the other from his heir Nanyue Huairang 南嶽懷讓 **(5.84)**. The more differentiated Chan thus emerging from the CDL was the product of a dynamic world in the ferment of a Renaissance. As a complex, subtle blend of Fayan and Linji Chan (belonging to the Qingyuan Xingsi and Nanyue Huairang lines respectively) it is a masterly literary monument to the skill of its redactors in creating a newly refurbished Chan school. Master Linji's school takes up books 6-13; Master Fayan's lineage from Huineng occupies books 14-26. The collateral branches are also recorded, the Niutou 牛頭 (Oxhead) school (Book 4), from the Fourth Patriarch Dao Xin 道信 **(3.41)** and the collateral branch from the Fifth Patriarch Hong Ren 弘忍 **(3.42),** the inheritors from the Northern School of Shenxiu 神秀 **(4.61)**.

Thereafter we are taken, via the transmission from Heart to Heart, up to the *Jingde* reign period (1004-10 CE) of the Song dynasty. The CDL records this sequential transmission, from one master to another across the generations. Not delineating a family tree as much as a web of relationships bound together by a particular approach to the perennial spiritual quest, the CDL does consist of individual biographies of various masters, yet the primary concern is to differentiate the religious practice that came to be known as 'Chan', whose description, at the beginning of the *Jingde* period (1004 CE), was still in an inchoate literary form. What the new homegrown 'Lamp' genre of Chan literature affords is a cohesive bird's-eye view of the web of spiritual affinities within the Chan School, independent of time and place. Chan called itself 'a special transmission outside the teachings' – it was accessible to all, monk and layman, to high and low, ancient and modern, to Confucians and Daoists, as well as to Buddhists of all Schools. As in any universal religion, the individual's personal history was not an important element; what counted was the golden thread of spiritual affinity.

These Records are not grim accounts of spiritual heroics, the battling against all odds to reach 'enlightenment'; rather they reveal the wonder of a direct re-linkage to the mystery of being alive, vividly experienced in a deep and joyous everyday life never far from physical hardships. The ultimate meaning of existence is revealed as simply fulfilling an innate human potential for re-linking to this quiet wonder, which we are time and again assured is everyone's birthright by virtue of being born human. If all things are in harmony at all times, as testified by the lives recorded in these Records, then this fact alone makes most of life unfathomable. Unfortunately, the decline of traditions of participation in this everyday wonder has today reduced life to a few stark realities that cause the heart to ache. The CDL is a call to remember, the only defence against the persistent impulse to forget. The universal guidelines it contains, tested and proved over the last fifteen hundred years, is called 'Chan' because they belong to the family of the Buddhas. Their obvious hope is to furnish the means of an initial re-linkage to the source of joy and free play, to the way out of suffering.

Concerning an eventual full return to the human Heart as it really is (the point of playing the Chan game) particularly tantalising is the account of the necessity of undertaking a further journey after re-linkage. The destination of this further journey is a world now seen from the fully humanised Heart as even beyond it, a veritable world where Heart is No-Heart – thus the optimal all-day-long playing conditions. The way to this world is to be found by trekking to the very centre of the Heart itself, where, according to the Records, there is an entrance to this other realm. The final negotiation of the passage that debouches into this new world where the game, in its most concrete form, is all that exists, is the crucial and in-depth realisation that the full return is to *this world, our world.* Here the spiritual life takes on the most convincing of all qualities, *solidity* and confers a sublime, everyday sense of *concreteness* – awareness at its most focused – to all activity.

Nor does the path come to an end: the ongoing maturation of a living being's potential, which has no set limits, is all that there is. Embedded in this living arena of open possibilities is the full realisation that life has no static goals at all since experience itself becomes continuous regeneration. Therefore any fixed view of existence is an abstraction contrary to reality; continual transformation, the ongoing dissolution of redundant structures, be they physical, emotional, mental or spiritual, is the only law.

Life is a web of connections complex enough to defy a definitive description – let alone understanding – so that all that can be said is actually another imposition and without intrinsic reality. Chan is a teaching developed for the purpose of breaking free from it, in order to participate in life's open-ended play. It is a map, drawn in one particular mode using a certain projection system that has no reality, depending as it does, on the particular projection used to develop the map. To verify the accuracy of the map for ourselves we need only walk this road taking the Patriarchs as our guides, armed with the perennial question – 'What is the meaning of the patriarch coming from, or *to*, the West?'

Abbreviations

Primary Sources:

DS – *Dong Chansi Ban* (Tōji) edition (1080 CE), The Eastern [Chan] Temple Edition [of the
CDL] 東禪寺版 edited by 四口芳男

FG – *Foguang Dazang Jing* 佛光大藏經, 1983

T – Taishō *Shinshū Daizōkyō* 大正新修大藏經常, 55 volumes, edited by Takakusu Junjirō and Watanabe Kaigyoku, (1912-1926). (The Taisho CDL, T.51, no.2076 is the Yuan edition published 1316/1360 CE based on the Sibu Congkan 四部叢刊, A Collection of The Four Branches of Literature of 1134 CE)

X – Shinsan Dainihon Zokuzokyo, 卍新纂大日本續藏經 Tokyo, Kokusho Kanokai, 東京, 國書刊行會

XY – *Xinyi Jingde Chuandeng Lu* 新譯經得傳燈錄 A New Translation of the Records of the Transmission of the Lamp, translated and annotated by Gu Hongyi 顧宏義, published by *Sanmin Shuju* 三民書局 Taibei, 2005. 3 vols. This edition is a collation based on the *Sibu Congkan* 四部叢刊 edition of 1134 and is the main source for the present translation.

ZTJ – *Zutang Ji* 祖堂集 Anthology from the Patriarchal Hall by *Jing* 靜 and *Jun* 筠 *Zhonghua Chuban* 中華出版, 2 vols. 2007

Secondary Sources:

Chinese:

ZGFJS – *Zhongguo Fojiao Shi* 中國佛教史 (History of Chinese Buddhism), by Ren Jiyu, 任繼愈, 3 vols. Beijing, 1981, 1985, 1988

Japanese:

KIK – *Kokuyaku issai-Kyō; Wa-kan senjutsu-bu* 國譯一切經 The Chinese and Japanese section of the Japanese Tripiṭaka, containing the Japanese translations of the Chinese Buddhist texts written in Kambun, with introductions and footnotes by Japanese scholars, vol. 82. Tokyo, 33rd year of the Shōwa 昭和 period (1959)

KDI – *Keitoku Dentoroku* 景德傳燈錄, books 7-12 annotated under the supervision of *Irya, Yoshitaka* 入矢義高昂, 2 vols, Kyoto, Institute of Zen Studies (Zenbunka Kenkyujo), 1993

KTS – *Keitoku Dentoroku Sakuin* 景德傳燈錄索引 compiled by 芳澤勝弘 *et al*, 2 vols. Kyoto, Zenbunka Kenkyujo, 1993

Western:

AUL – *Jingde chuandeng lu. Aufzeichnungen von der Übertragung der Leuchte aus der Ära Jingde*, by Christian Wittern, Insel, 2014

BCA – *Buddhism in Central Asia*, by B. N. Puri, Delhi, 1987

BCC – *The Buddhist Conquest of China*, by E. Zürcher, Leiden, 1972

BCR – *The Blue Cliff Record*, translated by Thomas and J.C. Cleary, 3 vols., Boulder, 1977

BDT – *Buddhism, Diplomacy, and Trade: The Realignment of Sino-Indian Relations, 600-1400*, by Tansen Sen, Honolulu, Hawai'i, 2003

BICC – *Buddhism in Chinese Society*, by Jacques Gernet, Columbia, 1995

BFSS – *Beacon Fire and Shooting Star: The Literary Culture of the Liang (502-557)*, by Xiaofei Tian, Cambridge, Mass., 2007

CBD – *A Chinese Biographical Dictionary*, by Herbert Giles, 1898, Rprt. Taipei, 1975

CL – *Chinese Letterkunde*, by Wilt Idem and Lloyd Haft, Amsterdam, 1985, (in Dutch)

DCBT – *Dictionary of Chinese Buddhist Terms*, by W.E. Soothill & L. Hodous, London, 1937

DOTIC – *A Dictionary of Official Titles in Imperial China,* by Charles O. Hucker, Stanford, 1985

DPPN – *Dictionary of Pali Proper Names*, by G.P. Malalasekera, London, 1974

GEB – *Geography of Early Buddhism,* by B. C. Law, London, 1932

HCB – *Handbook of Chinese Buddhism,* by E.J. Eitel, Hong Kong, 1888

HCC – *A History of Chinese Civilization,* by Jacques Gernet, Cambridge, 1982

HIB – *A History of Indian Buddhism,* by Etienne Lamotte, translated by Sara Webb-Boin, Louvain, 1988

HRFD – *Historical Records of the Five Dynasties,* by Ouyang Xiu, translated by Richard L. Davies, Columbia, 2004

IB – *Indian Buddhism,* by Hajime Nakamura, Delhi, 1987

MRL – *Monks, Rulers, and Literati: The Political Ascendancy of Chan Buddhism*, by Albert Welter, Oxford, 2006

MT – The *Mystique of Transmission,* by Wendi L. Adamek, New York, 2007

NJ – *A Catalogue of the Chinese Translation of the Buddhist Tripiṭaka,* by Bunyiu Nanjio, Oxford, 1883

PSSP – *The Platform Sutra of the Sixth Patriarch,* by Philip B. Yampolsky, Columbia, 1967

SBCR – *Secrets of the Blue Cliff Record. Zen Comments by Hakuin and Tenkei,* translated by Thomas Cleary, Boston, 2000

SH – *A Study of History,* by Arnold Toynbee, 12 vols. Oxford, 1934-61, Rprt. 1979

TZC – *Two Zen Classics,* translated by Katsuki Sekida, New York, 1977; rprt., 1985

YCB – *Das Yulu des Chan-Buddhismus: Die Entwicklung vom 8.-11. Jahrhundert am Beispiel des 28. Kapitels des Jingde chuandenglu (1004)* by Christian Wittern, Bern, 1998

ZS – *Zen Sand,* by Victor Sogen Hori, Hawai'i, 2003

Book One

The Seven Buddhas:
(in Chinese, **Sanskrit** and *Japanese*)

1.1 Pipo Shi Fo (**Vipashin Buddha**) *(Bibashi Butsu)*
1.2 Shiqi Fo (**Shikhin Buddha**) *(Shiki Butsu)*
1.3 Pishe Fu Fo (**Vishvabhu / Vessabhū Buddha**) *(Bishafu Butsu)*
1.4 Juliu Sun Fo (**Krakucchanda / Kakusandha Buddha**) *(Kuruson Butsu)*
1.5 Juna Hanmuni Fo (**Kanakamuni / Konāgamana Buddha**) *(Kunagon-muni Butsu)*
1.6 Jiaye Fo (**Kāśyapā / Kassapa Buddha**) *(Kasho Butsu)*
1.7 Shijia Muni Fo (**Shakyamuni / Gotama Buddha**) *(Shakamuni Butsu)*

The Twenty-Eight Indian Patriarchs:

1.8 The 1st Patriarch Mohe Jiaye (**Mahākāśyapā**) *(Makkakasho Sonja)*
1.9 The 2nd Patriarch Anan (**Ānanda**) *(Anan Sonja)*
1.10 The 3rd Patriarch Shangna Hexiu, (**Sanakavāsa**) *(Shonawashu Sonja)*
1.11 The 4th Patriarch Jupo Jiuduo, (**Upagupta**) *(Ubakikuta Sonja)*
1.12 The 5th Patriarch Tiduo Jia, (**Dhritaka**) *(Daitaka Sonja)*
1.13 The 6th Patriarch Mizhe Jia, (**Michaka**) *(Mishaka Sonja)*
1.14 The 7th Patriarch Poxumi, (**Vasumitra**) *(Bashumitsu Sonja)*
1.15 The 8th Patriarch Fotuo Nanti, (**Buddhanandi**) *(Buddanandai Sonja)*
1.16 The 9th Patriarch Fotuo Miduo, (**Buddhamitra**) *(Fukudamitta Sonja)*
1.17 The 10th Patriarch Xiezun Zhe, (**Parsva**) *(Koke Zonsho Sonja)*
1.18 The 11th Patriarch Danna Yeshe, (**Punyayasas**) *(Funayasha Sonja)*
1.19 The 12th Patriarch Maming Dashi, (**Aśvagoṣa**) *(Memyo Sonja)*
1.20 The 13th Patriarch Jiapi Moluo, (**Kapimala**) *(Kabimora Sonja)*
1.21 The 14th Patriarch Lungshu Dashi, (**Nāgārjuna**) *(Ryuju Sonja)*

Preface

Preface to the Records of the Transmission of the Lamp [up to] the Jingde reign period [of the Song Dynasty 1004 CE].

Composed by Yang Yi[103], Hanlin Academician, Grand Master of the Closing Court, of the Office of Remonstrations, Drafter [of Imperial Documents], Associate of the State Historiographer, Supervisor in the Institute for the Advancement of Literature, Pillar of the State, Territorial Administrator to Nanyang, Dynasty-founding Marquis, Land-grant Noble, Recipient of the Golden Seal and the Purple Ribbon.[104]

In ancient times Shakyamuni, by receiving the cherished prediction of Buddhahood from Dipankara Buddha, became the next incumbent of this Good Kalpa.

Subduing the spirits, he taught and practiced for forty-nine years, opening the gates to the expedient, the real, the sudden and the gradual Ways, handing down the lesser, the greater, the partial and the complete teachings. Students awoke to the principle according to their understanding and thus there came into existence the difference between the three vehicles. Bringing concrete advantages to life, he also conducted innumerable people [to the other shore]. Vast and great indeed was his compassion, the form of his rule complete in everything. Entering cessation at the twin trees, only *Mahākāśyapā* was considered [worthy to receive the transmission].

The fine robe was later transmitted firstly to Bodhidharma

Not standing on the written word,
Directly pointing to the source of the Heart
Not stepping up any ladders
But a direct ascent to the Buddha-land.

---

[103] 974-1030 CE. A Vice-Chancellor of the Hanlin Academy employed in preparing the dynastic annals. CBD: 2387.

[104] All these titles are to be found in Hucker, DOTIC.

Spreading into five branches[105] the teaching flourished and dividing into a thousand lamps it prospered. Those who reached the precious place were therefore many and those turning the Dharma-wheel were not few. The purport entrusted by the Great Hero and the Way circulated by the ones who see properly is the teaching beyond other practices, which cannot be fathomed.

Since the time of the sacred Song the human spirit has been profoundly nurtured. Emperor Taizu[106] has suppressed rebellions with his spiritual power, in order to reverence purity and endow Buddhist temples, thus opening the gateway to salvation. Emperor Taizong,[107] with imperial intelligence and royal eloquence, explained the true doctrine clearly. Our present Emperor,[108] with divine sagacity, has pursued the literary work of his father by a preface to the sacred scriptures, clarifying the religious style, illumining the cloudy chapters in the heaven of understanding and raising the golden voice in the garden of enlightenment. In intimate harmony with the words in the Lotus treasury, the clue from India and Gandhara was able to prosper, so that those sowing good seeds flourish mightily. The ones who transmit the full meaning appear from time to time and the influence of the complete and sudden has flowed even into our region.

In eastern Wu there was a Buddhist monk named Daoyuan, deep-hearted and delighting in Chan, who investigated the profound school of the void and unravelled the great genealogies of the patriarchs. He collected the recorded dialogues from all schools and arranging the order of the originals, synthesised their confused sentences. From the seventh Buddha to the heirs of the great Fayan, one thousand seven hundred and one persons, from fifty-two generations, have been collected in thirty books which have been entitled *Records of the Transmission of the Lamp to the Jing De period*. Respectfully approaching the Imperial court in the hope of publishing them, the Emperor, considering himself exceptionally placed to protect the Buddha-dharma, commended the strenuous work of this Buddhist monk and, having pondered deeply for a year

[105] The Five Houses of Chan (五家) arose in during the Tang dynasty (618-905 CE). They were the Linji (臨濟宗), Caodong (曹洞宗), Guiyang (潙仰宗), Yunmen (雲門宗) and Fayan (法眼) branches, named after their respective founders.

[106] 927-976 CE, Founder of the Song dynasty.

[107] Brother of Taizu, second emperor of the Song dynasty, 939-997 CE, who came to the throne in 976.

[108] Emperor Zhenzong ascended the Imperial throne in 998 CE.

and exercised His power of thought for a long time, He decreed that his humble servants, Yang Yi, Hanlin Academician, of the Left Office of the Department of State Affairs, Drafter to the Office of Remonstrator, and Li Wei of the Ministry of War, vice-director of the Imperial Department of Drafters, together with Wang Shu, an Aide in the Chamberlain's Office for Ceremonials – and others – should edit the book. However, we servants are ignorant of the purport of the Three Learnings,[109] confused concerning aspects of the Five Natures,[110] and deficient in the ability to translate smoothly, being muddle-headed about the importance of silence in regard to the difference between the Twelve Divisions of the Buddhist Canon and of heretical theories. Respectfully receiving the august command we did not dare but yield anxiously and so engaged in deep investigation without rest.

The criteria for these selections therefore was to take true emptiness as the fundamental, by a description of how the sages of former times nurtured the Way, as well as showing how the works of the men of old were in accord with the Principle. Fortuitous causes clash like the points of arrows on a battlefield and the store of Wisdom unites rays of light, casting the shadows of whips which stimulate the students who come later to spread the free-flowing profound Way by taking it up themselves.

Yet the examples and quotations that have been published contain many dregs, so that the essential oil has to be sought for. When there was the Great Master to show the Way to followers, they spoke with one voice, began to practice and cherished the urge to listen, as thousands of sages have born witness. And even a few examples of these cases will be helpful, though if any embellishments are added crucial points might be lost. The problem is not the difference between the Indian and Chinese languages so much as the risk of cutting a precious stone in the wrong way.

Again, all the cases being from antiquity, the verity of the facts recorded must therefore rest on good reports. Stories that have travelled far should not be lacking in documentation, should show the actual provenance of the records with detailed statements as to their origins. Both the confused threads of a disorderly collection and words that had become enmeshed in vulgar expressions have all been cut out in order to penetrate through.

---

[109] Confucianism, Daoism and Buddhism.
[110] The *five natures* (五性 *wu xing*) are (1) Bodhisattvas, (2) Śravakas and Pratyekabuddhas, (3) ordinary good people, (4) agnostics, (5) heretics, DCB:118.

When it comes to dialogues with well-known Confucian officials of rank, we have checked their official careers and have deleted all inaccuracies in the light of traditional verities. If we ourselves contribute a spark of profound interest, then the swift movement of lightening, which shows the true heart's miraculous clarity, will suddenly be aroused. The Patriarchs declare the deep truth of the emptiness of suffering, so how can we, in harmony with the metaphor of the transmission of a lamp, claim the merit of scraping away the membrane [of blindness]?

If there is only a description of the response of being touched by spells and omens, or the exclusive narration of the accounts of pilgrimages, then these have already been recorded in the biographies of monks. Again, why take to explanations of Chan? The purpose here is to preserve the natural transmission from Master to Master recorded in the old records. Although some are bulky and lack the essence, other collections are very compact, thus the need to search for documents and to make good any deficiencies generally, by adding context to the collections.

The work's preface may not be the work of the old masters, but to inquire into the proper order and comment on everything would only add redundancies, so by judicious selection much has also been cut.

About a year having past, the writing is finished. Your humble servants' natural understanding is shameful in its stupidity, humiliating in its shallowness, their springs of divine action mediocre and their literary ability without distinction.

The Wonderful Way rests with men and although we cleaned our hearts out for a long time, still the profound words are not accessible to average beings, and we have often been confronted with a blank wall.

The bias of the selection being excessive, there was no fulfilling the direction to publish and having been unable to bring to an end a refined explanation, we respectfully present the work to the Imperial leisure, yet without having had the assistance of the Imperial scholarship, which perceives the empty dust [of our efforts] with divine sagacity. Respectfully we present this endeavour to the throne.

Concerning the Seven Buddhas[111]

The ancient Buddhas have responded to the world for an immeasurable length of time without break, so it is impossible to enumerate them all.

Talking only of this Good Kalpa,[112] it will have one thousand Tathāgata's. Only seven, up to Shakyamuni are recorded here. According to the *Dīrghāgama Sutra* 'the power of right effort of the Seven Buddhas radiated light, thus banishing the darkness, and each sat under a tree and attained perfect awakening. Manjuśri was the Founding Father [of their teaching].'

When the great layman Shanhui of Jinhua[113] climbed to the top of Song Mountain[114] to practice the Way, he felt the Seven Buddhas leading ahead and Vimalakirti[115] following behind. For the present anthology therefore Seven Buddhas have been selected, as below.

1.1 Vipashin Buddha[116] was the 998th Buddha of the previous *kalpa* called Stately and Dignified.[117]

---

[111] The Seven Buddhas – this copies the list given in the *Mahāpadāna Suttanta* [The Sublime Story] from the *Dīgha Nikāya*, D.ii.2, ff. See the English translation in *'Dialogues of the Buddha'*, Vol. II, translated from the Pali by T.W. & C.A.F. Rhys Davids, 1910, p. 4-41 (in *The Sacred Books of the East Series*, Vol. III).

[112] Good Kalpa – Pali, *Bhadda-Kappa*, a *kalpa* such as the present one in which one thousand Buddhas are or will be born. DCBT: 444b; DPPN:II, 349.

[113] For more on Shanhui, 497-569 CE, a noted follower of Bodhidharma, see *Chan and Zen Teaching*, First Series by Lu K'uan Yu (Charles Luk). Rider, 1960, pp.143-5.

[114] The first mention of Song Mountain, the later location of the Shaolin Temple of Bodhidharma.

[115] A semi-mythological Buddhist layman and bodhisattva said to be living in Vaishali at the time of the Buddha, after whom a Mahāyāna *sutra* is named (*Vimalakirti Nirdesa Sutra* – see *L'Enseignement de Vimalakirti*, translated by Etienne Lamotte. Louvain, 1962, re-translated into English by Sarah Boin).

[116] DPPN: II, 886.

[117] A *kalpa* is said to be 320 million years long, a great kalpa, such as the previous one, 1,980 million years. See further Cheetham, E. *Fundamentals of Mainstream Buddhism*. Grove Editions, 1996, p. 17.

His *gatha* reads:

The body undergoes birth from the midst of no-form
Like a mirage emerging from various shapes;
The heart of a mirage-man knows that originally there is nothing,
Bad fortune or good, both are empty for there is no resting-place.[118]

The *Dīrghāgama Sutra* says, 'In the time when men lived for eighty thousand years, this Buddha appeared in the world. He was of the noble cast and his surname was Kondana, his father's name was Badhuma, his mother's Bandhumati and he lived in the city of Bandhumati.

He sat under a Phalassa Tree and expounded the Dharma three times, leading three times four hundred and eighty thousand persons to the other shore. His two chief disciples were Khanda and Tissa, his attendant was Aśoka and his son was Samadattakkhandha.'

1.2 Sikhin Buddha[119] was the 999th Buddha of the previous *kalpa*, Stately and Dignified.

His *gatha* reads:

All the good dharmas which arise are originally a mirage
The production of all evil *karma* is likewise a mirage.
The body is like a collection of bubbles, the heart like the wind
The mirage that emerges has no root, no real nature.

In the *Dīrghāgama Sutra* it says, 'In the time when men lived for seventy thousand years this Buddha appeared in the world. He was of the noble cast and his family name was Kondanna. His father's name was Aruna, his mother's Pathavati and he lived in the city of Arunavati. He sat under a white lotus tree and expounded the Dharma on three occasions, leading two hundred and fifty thousand persons to the other shore. His two chief disciples were Abhibhu and Sambhava. His attendant was Khemenkara and his son Atula.'

---

[118] Compare the rendition of these *gathas* with a translation and commentary of the same by Lu K'uan Yu (Charles Luk) in *Chan and Zen Teaching (*Second Series). Rider, 1961, pp.27-53.
[119] DPPN: II, 1130.

1.3 Vishvabhu Buddha[120] was the 1000th Buddha of the previous *kalpa*, Stately and Dignified.

His *gatha* reads:

Borrowing from the four great elements to make the body,
The heart, originally birthless, exists due to circumstances;
Before circumstances came to exist the heart didn't exist either
Bad fortune or good are like mirages, they arise and they perish.

In the *Dīrghāgama Sutra* it says, 'In the time when men lived to be sixty thousand years old this Buddha appeared in the world. He was of the noble cast and his family name was Kondanna. His father's name was Suppatita, his mother's Yasavati and he lived in the city of Anopama. He sat under a Phala tree and expounded the Dharma on two occasions, leading one hundred and thirty thousand persons to the other shore. His two chief disciples were Sona and Uttara, his attendant Upasannaka and his son was Suppabuddha.'

1.4 Krakucchanda Buddha[121] was the first Buddha of this present *kalpa* called Auspicious.

His *gatha* reads:

Seeing the body as insubstantial, this is the Buddha-body
Understanding the heart to be like a mirage is the mirage of Buddha.
Having come to understand both body and heart
As being in their original nature empty,
How is such a man different from Buddha?

In the *Dīrghāgama Sutra* it says, 'In the time when men lived to be forty thousand years old this Buddha appeared in the world. He was of the *Brahmin* cast and his family name was Kāśyāpa. His father's name was Aggidatta, his mother's Visakha. He lived in the city of Khemavati, sat under a Sirissa tree and expounded the Dharma on one occasion, leading forty thousand persons to the other shore. The two chief disciples were Sanjiva and Vidhura and his son was Uttara.'

[120]DPPN: II, 947.
[121]DPPN: I, 470.

1.5 Kanakamuni Buddha[122] was the second Buddha of the present *kalpa*, Auspicious.

His *gatha* reads:

Buddha's invisible body is known as Buddha –
If this is truly known then there is no other Buddha.
The wise one can discern the nature of retribution to be empty,
At ease, he is not afraid of life or death.

In the *Dīrghāgama Sutra* it says, 'In the time when men lived to be thirty thousand years old this Buddha appeared in the world. He was of the *Brahmin* cast and his family name was Kāśyapā. His father's name was Yannadatta, his mother's Uttar and he lived in the city of Sobhavati. He sat under a fig tree and expounded the Dharma on one occasion, leading thirty thousand persons to the other shore. His two chief disciples were Bhiyosa and Uttara. His attendant was Sutthija and his son was called Sattavaha.'

1.6 Kāśyapā Dasabala Buddha[123] was the third Buddha of the present *kalpa* called Auspicious.

His *gatha* reads:

The nature of all sentient beings is pure.
From original birthlessness there is no death
Therefore this body and heart is illusorily born
In illusory transformations there is no bad fortune or good.

In the *Dīrghāgama Sutra* it says, 'In the time when men lived to be twenty thousand years old this Buddha appeared in the world. He was of the *Brahmin* cast and his family name was Kāśyapā. His father was Brahmadatta, his mother Dhanavati. He lived in the city of Baranasi and sat under a Banyan tree and expounded the Dharma on one occasion, when he led twenty thousand persons to the other shore. His two chief disciples were Tissa and Bhardaraja. His attendant was Sabhamitta and his son was Vijitasena.'

---

[122] DPPN: I, 681.
[123] DPPN: I, 546.

1.7   Shakyamuni Buddha[124] was the fourth Buddha of the present *kalpa* called Auspicious.

He was of the noble cast and his father was named Suddhodana.[125] His mother was Maya.[126] His rank having been elevated to that of occupying the place of a future Buddha he was born in the *Tushita* Heaven[127] under the name of Heavenly Being of Surpassing Virtue, also called Great Master Guardian of the Light, where he led many heavenly beings to the other shore, expounding the practice of 'taking up ones proper stature', his body also appearing in all the ten directions when expounding the Dharma.

In the *Lalitavistara*[128] it says, 'The Buddha was first born into a noble royal family, releasing the great light of wisdom into every direction of the universe. The earth gave rise to golden lotus blossoms naturally supporting his feet. Taking seven steps to the four directions of East, West, South and North, and with one hand pointing to heaven, the other to earth, he emitted the great lion's roar – "above and below and in all the directions, I alone am worthy of reverence".'[129] This took place during the reign of King Zhao of the Zhou dynasty, on the eighth day of April in the twenty-sixth year of his reign, corresponding to the fifty-first year of the sexagenarian cycle.[130]

Coming to the forty-fourth year [of the same reign], on the eighth day of February, [the crown prince, Gautama], in his nineteenth year, wishing to explore beyond his home thought to himself, 'What might I come across out there?' and wandering forth from the four [palace] gates beheld four things. In

[124]DPPN: I, 788 under 'Gotama'.

[125]DPPN: II, 1200.

[126]DPPN: II, 608.

[127]The fourth *Deva Loka* of the six heavens of desire, where all future Buddhas are reborn before descending to earth as Buddhas; the life in *Tushita* (*Tush* means contented, satisfied) lasts for 4,000 *Tushita* years, or – each day being equal to 400 earth years – 584 million earth years. *Tushita* is situated in between the *Yama* and *Nirmānarati* Heavens and its inner chamber is the Pure Land of Maitreya. DCBT: 343a.

[128] First translated into Chinese in 212 CE, now lost; later translated by Dharmaraksha in 308 CE, being the story of Shakyamuni's life. T.186, Nanjio. 160; T.187. Nj.159.

[129]The lion's roar is a metaphor for the majesty and power of a Buddha's spiritual presence when giving voice to the Dharma, a sound which causes the whole cosmos to tremble sympathetically.

[130] These dates are not to be taken historically.

his heart was the warmth of compassion that caused him to ponder deeply, saying, 'This old age, sickness and death can ultimately be done away with.' That
night a heavenly being named 'Pure Dwelling' came and respectfully saluting
the crown prince, said to him, 'The time to leave home has come – you can go.'
On hearing this, the crown prince's heart became supremely joyful and he leapt
away beyond the city, to the Kashmir Mountains,[131] in search of the Way.

First, at Ājāra Kālāma's place[132] he practiced the samādhi of non-action, but
knew that it would not fulfil his needs and rejected it. Then, coming to Uddaka
Rāmaputta's place[133] he practiced for three years the samādhi of 'neither perceptions nor non-perceptions' and came to know that it too was not the thing he
was seeking, so again rejected it. Then he came to Xiangtou Mountain[134] and
together with many heretics practiced for six years eating only gruel every day.

An old *sutra* says that, 'Without any heartfelt intentions or deliberate action
he completely subdued all the heretics.' When wrong teachings first occurred,
he put them to the test and showed them up with ease, enabling people to come
to *bodhi*. The *Lalitavistara Sutra* says that, 'In the twelfth month, on the eighth
day, at the time of the appearance of the morning star, the bodhisattva became a
Buddha called "the teacher of Gods and Men".' At that time he was thirty years
old, which was in the fourth year of the reign of King Mu, corresponding to the
twentieth year of the sexagenarian cycle.

After this, in the Deer Park, he turned the Dharma-wheel of the Four
Noble Truths for the sake of Anna-Kondanna[135] and the rest of the five ascetics,

---

[131] Tan Te Shan, Dantaloka, a mountain 'near Varucha' with a cavern (now called the
Kashmiri Ghar) where Sudāna (a previous incarnation of Buddha, DCBT: 395a), or
some say Siddhartha, underwent his ascetic practices. (DCBT:458b).

[132] DPPN:I, 296.

[133] DPPN: I, 383.

[134] Gaya Shiras, 'Elephant (*gaya*) Head Mountain', near Gayā, DCBT:390. Gayā is 12km.
north of Bodhgaya. See also *Where the Buddha Walked: A Companion to the Buddhist
Places of India* by Rana P.B.Singh. Varanasi, 2003, pp. 104-19.

[135] DPPN: I, 43, or Ajñāta Kaundinya, uncle and first cousin of Shakyamuni, the first human
to hear the Dharma; together with the other four, the group came to be known as the
Pancavaggiyā ('belonging to a group of five', DPPN: II, 104). The other four were: Bhad-
diya (II, 359?), Vappa, (II, 832), Mahānāma, (II, 513[2]) and Assaji (I, 224). To this group
the Buddha preached his first sermon – the *Dhammacakkappa Vattana Sutta*, then the
Anattalakkhana Sutta, at Isipatana (DPPN: I, 323) on the full-moon day of Aasālha =
June-July: all became *Arahants*. Assaji was responsible for Sariputra's conversion, with

expounding the Way and its Fruition. He taught the Dharma whilst living in the world for forty-nine years. Then he said to his disciple Mahākāśyapā, 'I now hand over to you the pure Dharma-eye of nirvāṇa, the miraculous heart, the true form-without-form, the delicate and wondrous True Dharma. You should guard it and uphold it.' Then he told Ānanda to assist with the transmission and not to allow it to go into decline, pronouncing the following:

His *gatha* reads,

Dharma's original Dharma is no-dharma
The Dharma of no-dharma is also a Dharma
When no-dharma is being transmitted
How could this Dharma of dharmas be a Dharma?

When he had finished reciting this *gatha* the World-Honoured One said once more to Mahākāśyapā, 'this golden brocaded robe I hand over to you: it should be passed on to all incumbent Buddhas until Maitreya Buddha appears in the world. Do not allow it to rot.'

Mahākāśyapā, having heard this utterance, made a prostration and said, 'It is well, it is well! I will reverently follow the Buddha according to his instructions.' At that time the World-Honoured One came to Kushinagārā,[136] where he said to the great congregation, 'Today I have a pain in my back and wish to enter nirvāṇa.' Then he went to the Sala trees[137] by the side of the Hirannavatī River.[138] Lying down on his right side, with one leg on the other, he entered peaceful cessation. Then once more he arose, from his coffin, for the sake of expounding the Dharma to his [deceased] mother,[139] and especially showed his feet to Poqi[140] for his salvation and expounded on Impermanence, with the *gatha*:

these words: 'of those things that arise from a cause, the Tathāgata has told the cause, and also what their cessation is: this is the doctrine of the Great Recluse'.

[136] I.e. (in Pali) Kusinārā, DPPN: I, 653, modern Kasiah, 180 miles NW of Patna; the place where Buddha Shakyamuni died. Together with Kapilavatthu, Buddhagayā, and Isipatana, the place became one of the four places of pilgrimage to be undertaken by a follower of Buddha's Law.

[137] *Shorea robusta*, the teak tree.

[138] In Pali, Hirannavatī, DPPN: II, 1327.

[139] Said to be residing in the *Tushita* Heaven.

[140] Unknown disciple of the Buddha.

All formations are impermanent
They are born and they die.
Having put an end to birth and death
Then peaceful cessation is happiness.

Then all the disciples at that time struggled to cremate him with scented firewood. When only the embers were left, the coffin was as before [the cremation]. Then the great assembly recited the following *gatha* in front of the Buddha:

The average man burns with a fierce blaze
Yet how can it bring about this burning [of the Buddha]?
May it be the World-Honoured One's Fire Samādhi
Which cremates the golden-coloured body!

At that time the golden coffin rose from its place to a height of seven palm trees, going back and forth in the air, transforming into the Fire Samādhi. In an instant only ash remained, producing eighty-four pecks of *śarīra* relics.[141] This was in the reign of King Mu, in his fifty-third year, on the fifteenth day of February, corresponding to the ninth year of the sexagenarian cycle.

One thousand one hundred and seventeen years after the demise of the World-Honoured One his teaching reached the Middle Kingdom; this was in the eleventh year of the Yongping reign period of the Later Han Dynasty, corresponding to the fifth year of the sexagenarian cycle [68 CE].

[141] The pearl or crystal-like bead-shaped essences of cremated Buddhist spiritual masters.

The Indian Patriarchs[142]

1.8   Mahākāśyapā,[143] the First Patriarch.

Mahākāśyapā was a native of Magadha and of the *Brahmin* cast. His father's name was Drinking of Grace, his mother's Incense Offerer. In a previous incarnation he had been a master goldsmith and knew well the nature of metals, which were malleable under his hands. In *The Transmission of the Dharma* it is said that once, in a *kalpa* long ago, after Vipashin Buddha had entered nirvāṇa, the four assemblies (of monks, nuns, layman and laywomen) had a *stupa* built. In the *stupa* there was a small defect on the face of the golden image. At that time a woman who was very poor took a gold bead to the goldsmith and asked him to repair the face of the Buddha with it.

After that, owing to their conceiving the wish, they entered into a spiritual marriage and because of this were reborn in the *Brahma* Heaven where for ninety-one *kalpas* their bodies were covered in gold. The heavenly term having been exhausted, the goldsmith was reborn into a *Brahmin* family in Magadha, Central India, with the name of Mahākāśyapā, which means, 'the triumphant honoured one who drinks light', probably taking his golden body as the queue. He wanted to seek the homeless life with the wish to save all sentient beings.

On the Buddha saying to him, 'Welcome monk,' he shaved off his own hair and beard and donned the robe. He was always praised as the first amongst the assembly. Later the Buddha said to him, 'I transmit to you the pure eye of the Dharma, may it spread far and wide through you. Do not let it perish.'

In the *Nirvāṇa Sutra* it says, 'At the time that the World-Honoured One wished to enter nirvāṇa Kāśyapā was not amongst the assembly. The Buddha told all the chief disciples, "When Kāśyapā arrives have him propagate the

---

[142] The first five patriarchs are not found in the Pali Canon or in the Singhalese tradition, though 'The Five Masters of the Law' as listed in *The Life of King Aśoka* and translated from Sanskrit into Chinese by An Fajin (265 – 319 CE) was an accepted tradition on mainland India. See T. 2042, Ch. 2-3, pp. 111b28-121b1, as well as lists in T. 1465 (Nj. 1152), a *Mahāsāmghika* list; T. 1451 (Nj.1121), a *Mūlasarvāstivādin* list; T. 618 (Nj. 1341), *Yogacarabhumi* by Buddhasena and others. See Lamotte, HIB: pp. 206-212; 690-699, from whose work this information and these references are taken.

[143] DPPN: II, 476.

Treasure of the True Dharma-eye".' At that time Kāśyapā was in the Pippala Cave on Binbo Luoku Mountain (Grdhrakuta Mountain, near Rajagrha). Gazing at a transcendent bright light he entered samādhi and saw, with the pure heavenly eye, the World-Honoured One entering nirvāṇa by the side of the Hirannavatī River. 'The Tathāgata's nirvāṇa, so soon!', he said to his followers. Arriving at the Sala trees he shed tears of affection. The Buddha's feet then appeared from the golden coffin.

At that time Kāśyapā told all the assembled monks, 'With the cremation of the Buddha the diamond *śarīra* relics are not our concern. It is fitting that we collect the Dharma-eye and not allow the teaching to decline.' Then he spoke the following *gatha*:

Oh disciples of the Tathāgata do not enter nirvāṇa.
Those who have attained spiritual transcendence
Should proceed to a meeting to collect the teachings.

All those who had attained transcendence then gathered at the Pippala Cave at the Binbo Luoku Mountain (Grdhrakuta) near Rajagrha. At that time Ānanda, because his passions were not yet exhausted, did not gain entry to the meeting. Later his *Arhatship* was confirmed and so he gained entry.

Kāśyapā then said to the assembly, 'This monk Ānanda has heard much and retained it all. He has great wisdom and was always accompanying the Tathāgata. Impeccable is his conduct and pure, so that hearing the Buddha's Dharma was like water that had been poured from one vessel into another without a drop being spilled. The Buddha praised him as being the first in intelligence. It would be proper therefore to ask him to collect the teachings.' The great assembly approved by remaining silent. Kāśyapā said to Ānanda, 'Today it is fitting that you proclaim [the teachings you have heard] with the Eye of the Dharma!'

Ānanda, having heard these words, faithfully accepted [the task]. Seeing clearly into the hearts of those assembled he pronounced this *gatha:*

Oh monks, separated from the Buddha
All our family is without adornment
Like the multitude of stars without a moon!

Having finished this *gatha* he prostrated himself before the assembly, ascended the Dharma-seat and spoke these words: 'Thus have I heard. At one time the Buddha was abiding at such-and-such a place and delivered such-and-such a teaching, so that men and gods made obeisance to him, wishing to practice the Dharma…'

Then Mahākāśyapā asked all the monks, 'Are the words of Ānanda false or not?' All replied, 'They are not different from the ones spoken by the World-Honoured One.'

Kāśyapā then said to Ānanda, 'I will not remain much longer this year, so I now hand over the true Dharma to you. Guard it well. Listen to my *gatha*:'

Each thing's original Dharma
Is neither a Dharma, nor a non-dharma
How could there be a Dharma or a non-dharma
In any dharma?

Having finished the *gatha*, holding the robe he entered Chicken Foot Mountain[144] waiting for the future birth of Maitreya. This was in the fifth year of the reign of King Xiao of the Zhou dynasty, corresponding to the fifty-third year of the sexagenarian cycle.

1.9   Ānanda, the Second Patriarch[145]

Ānanda, the second patriarch, was from Rajagrha and his family was of the noble cast. His father was King Amitodana,[146] so he was a real cousin of the Buddha. In the language of Sanskrit 'Ānanda' means 'joyful', also 'to like'. He was born on the night that the Tathāgata attained to the Way [under the *Bodhi* tree], thus his name. Through much listening he became learned and his wisdom was unobstructed. Of all the World-Honoured One's attendants he was praised as the foremost, having accumulated great merit during previous lives. He could receive and retain the treasure of the Dharma, like water [poured from one vessel into another] so the Buddha trained him as his attendant.

In later times King Ajātasatru asked Ānanda, saying, 'Venerable Sir, the Tathāgata and Kāśyapā, when these two honoured and victorious masters came

---

[144] In Magadha.
[145] DPPN: I, 249.
[146] DPPN: I, 148.

to the end in nirvāṇa, I, because of many matters, was unable to see them. When the time comes for the Venerable Sir's nirvāṇa may he deign to say farewell?' Ānanda agreed to this. When [Ānanda] later came to the thought that 'my body is as fragile as a bubble and moreover it's getting old – why put up with such a long life any longer?', he remembered his promise to King Ajātasatru and went to the palace to tell the king, saying to the gatekeeper, 'I will enter nirvāṇa and have come to take my leave.' But the gatekeeper said, 'The king is asleep. He cannot give you a hearing.' So Ānanda said, 'When His Majesty wakes up later, convey my message.' At that same moment King Ajātasatru saw, in a dream, a precious canopy decorated with seven precious treasures and surrounded by millions of admirers. Suddenly a ferocious storm blew up, broke the canopy supports and all the priceless ornaments crashed to the ground. His heart was startled and so he woke up. The gatekeeper then told him the above news and after he heard it [the King] lost his senses and cried in extreme grief, deep as the universe. He proceeded at once to Vaishali, where he saw Ānanda crossing the Ganges River, sitting cross-legged [on a boat]. Bowing in respectful greeting, the King then recited the following *gatha*:

Adoration to the Honoured One in the Triple World!
Having come here, you are abandoning me!
For a time, according to the strength of your compassion
Please do not [enter] nirvāṇa!

The King of Vaishali was also there, on the other bank of the River Ganges and also recited the following *gatha*:

Oh Honoured One
Why are you so quickly
Returning to the peaceful place?
Remain here for a while
And receive our homage.

At that time Ānanda, who saw that both kings had arrived and were pleading passionately, spoke the following *gatha*:

Oh ye two kings,
Abide in goodness and majesty

Do not lament bitterly.
Take it from me –
Nirvāṇa is all calm,
For all that exists is nothing.

Then Ānanda thought to himself, 'If I am biased towards one kingdom and enter nirvāṇa then the others will contend and fight. Is there not a way to solve this? It is necessary that all have an equal opportunity to gain salvation.' Then he entered cessation in the middle of the Ganges River. At the same instant the mountains, the river and the great earth trembled in six ways. In the snowy mountains (Himalayas) were five hundred adepts who saw this auspicious omen and responded by flying through the air and arriving [immediately]. Prostrating themselves at Ānanda's feet in the manner of the northern barbarians, they said, 'We would like to witness the Buddha-dharma through the Venerable Sir, so please extend your great compassion to liberate us.'

Ānanda silently accepted the request. Then he changed the whole of the Ganges River into a field of gold and expounded all the Great Dharmas for the sake of these hermits. Again Ānanda thought of the disciples he had first liberated – that they too should come – and in a moment five hundred *Arhats* came down from the sky to officiate at these hermit's receiving of the ten pre-cepts ordination. There were two *Arhats* among them, one whose name was Sōnavāsa[147] and the other whose name was Madhyāntika[148] and knowing that they were vessels of the Dharma Ānanda said to them, 'In days gone by the Tathāgata transmitted the great Dharma-eye to Mahākāśyapā and when he entered cessation he transmitted it to me. I now, about to enter cessation, hand it over to you. You who receive my teaching should listen to this *gatha*:'

Originally handed down is the Dharma
Having been handed down it is called no-dharma
Everyone must awaken to it themselves
Having awoken to it nothing is not Dharma.

Ānanda, having transmitted the treasury of the Dharma-eye in its entirety, rose

---

[147] The future third patriarch. (DCBT.344a).
[148] One of the two chief disciples of Ānanda to whom he handed down the Buddha's Dhar-ma (DCBT.191b).

up in the air and went through the eighteen transformations[149] and then entered the wind-fury samādhi, dividing his body into four parts: one part to the Heaven of the Thirty-three;[150] one part to the Palace of Sāgara Dragon;[151] one to King Vaishali; one to King Ajātasatru. They erected a jewelled *stupa*, providing it with offerings.

This was in the eleventh year of King Li's reign, corresponding to the thirtieth year of the sexagenarian cycle.

1.10   Sanakavāsa, the Third Patriarch[152]

Sanakavāsa, the third patriarch, was from the country of Mathura.[153] He was also called Sannavasika and the family belonged to the merchant class. His father's name was Lin Sheng, his mother's, Jiao Sheye.

He was six years in the womb before emerging into the world. From the Sanskrit, 'Shangno Jia' means 'natural robe', which is to say, it was the name of a nine-tufted fine grass in India. When an *Arhat* or sage descended into birth this grass would grow on pure ground, which happened at the time of Sanakavāsa's birth when the auspicious grass manifested just like this.

In earlier times, when the Tathāgata was teaching in Mathura, he saw a verdant forest with luxurious vegetation and said to Ānanda, 'This forest will be called Uruda. One hundred years after my demise there will be a monk, Sanakavāsa, who will turn the wonderful Wheel of the Dharma on this spot.' Sure enough, after one hundred years Hexiu was born. He left the home life to live the authentic Way and received the transmission from the Venerable Ānanda and liberated sentient beings.

Having entered this forest he subdued two fiery dragons so that they took refuge in the Buddha-dharma. Because of this the dragons donated this ground to the founding of a Buddhist temple.

---

[149] A samādhi in which the whole body is conceived of as scattered, (DCBT.3118a).

[150] *Trayastrimsas* is the heaven of the thirty-three Devas and the second desire heaven of Indra. (DCBT.188b).

[151] Sāgara, a Nāga King of the Ocean Palace of Priceless Pearls, whose daughter instantly attained Buddhahood (chapter XI in the *Lotus Sutra* and DCBT. 323b).

[152] '...born 100 years after the nirvāṇa, identified with Yas'as, leader of the second synod' HCB:146.

[153] Modern Uttar Pradesh, North-west India, one of the seven holiest places for Hindus.

After the Master had been teaching for a long time he thought about the transmission of the True Dharma. He went in search to Pātaliputra and there came across Upagupta, whom he made his attendant. Then he asked Upagupta, 'How old are you?'

'I am seventeen,' he replied.

'Is it your body that is seventeen,' asked the master, 'or is your nature seventeen?'

Upagupta replied, 'The master's hair is already white, is that because the hair is white or because the heart is white?'

'Only my hair is white, the heart is not white,' replied the master.

'My body is seventeen,' said Upagupta, 'the nature is not seventeen.' Sanakavāsa knew then that [Upagupta] was a vessel of the Dharma and after three years he shaved his head and gave him the precepts.

One day Sanakavāsa said to Upagupta, 'In days gone by the Tathāgata transmitted the Treasury of the Supreme Dharma-eye to Mahākāśyapā. From him it was transmitted from one to another until it passed to me and I now transmit this to you; do not let it disappear. You, who have received my teaching, listen now to my *gatha*:'

It is neither a dharma nor a heart
For neither heart nor dharma exist
When talking of heart and dharma
This Dharma is not the heart or the dharma.

Having finished this *gatha* he secreted himself in the White Elephant Mountains in Kashmir. Later, whilst in samādhi, he saw that Upagupta's five hundred disciples were often extremely negligent. The master then immediately went into the 'aroused dragon' samādhi and through this transformation made them yield by reciting this *gatha*:

Unobstructed, it is not a this or a that.
Having come to sagehood,
It is without length or breadth.
If you get rid of facile meanings
Arhatship is swiftly attained.

After the five hundred had heard this *gatha*, they respectfully practiced by relying on this teaching and all came to [the state of being] without outflows. The master then performed the eighteen transformations of the fire-light samādhi and then cremated himself. Upagupta collected the *śarīra* relics and buried them in the Brahmakala Mountains. Five hundred monks came in procession, each with a banner, and there they built a *stupa* for offerings.

This took place in the twenty-third year of King Xuan, corresponding to the thirty-second year of the sexagenarian cycle.

1.11   Upagupta, the Fourth Patriarch.

Upagupta, the fourth patriarch, was a native of the kingdom of Pātaliputra. His other name was Yupo Jueduo and he also bore the name Wupo Guduo. His family was of the peasant class and the father was called Shaoyi (Good Will). At the age of seventeen he ordained as a monk and at twenty bore witness to the truth.

Teaching the Dharma everywhere, he arrived in the kingdom of Mathurā and there obtained the liberation of very many people, causing Mara's[154] palace to tremble. The Evil One was worried and consequently devoted all his dark powers to the harming of the True Dharma. The master then entered samādhi to investigate the cause [of the trouble]. The Evil One, spying on him, was stealthily holding a precious jade necklace, which he then slipped around Upagupta's neck. The master, arising out of samādhi, then took three corpses – that of a man, a dog and a snake – and transformed them into a beautiful garland. Speaking mild and assuaging words, the Master said to the Evil One, 'You have given me a precious necklace of value most rare. With this beautiful garland, I for my part would respectfully like to reciprocate.' The Evil One was greatly pleased and accepted the gift by extending his neck. Instantly the garland changed into three foul corpses, over-ripe with worms and maggots. The Evil One was disgusted and very angry. Even with the exhaustion of his spiritual strength through rage and sadness he was unable to extricate himself. Then he went up through all the six heavens of desire, telling all the heavenly kings about what had happened. He even went to Brahma in search of release from his difficulty. Each of those said, 'This spiritual transformation was executed by a disciple of the [the Buddha with the] ten powers; how can low ranking commoners dispatch the deed?' The Evil One said, 'This being so, what to do now?'

---

[154]The Buddhist Evil One.

Then *Brahma* said, 'You should take refuge in the Venerable Master who can remove it,' and recited a *gatha* to cause [the Evil One's] return to heel:

If one falls because of gravity
Then by gravity one has to get up;
Seeking to rise without using gravity
Is ultimately unreasonable.

The Evil One accepted this pointer and so descended from the Palace of Heaven. He prostrated himself at the Master's feet and, showing regret, repented. Upagupta said, 'Will you, from now on, continue to do harm to the True Dharma of the Tathāgata or not?'

'I vow to turn to the Buddha's way,' replied the Evil One, 'and will forever cease from not doing good.'

'If this be so,' said Upagupta, 'then you may chant aloud that you take refuge in the Three Jewels.'[155]

Mara, palms together, chanted. The necklace perished completely and with great joy and happiness he bowed to the master and recited a *gatha*:

Adoration to the Master of the three samādhis,
To the sage disciple of the ten powers.
Today I wish to turn to him
Without countenancing the existence
Of any meanness or weakness.

When the Master was in the world he guided many to the attainment of the fruit. For each one who had crossed to the other shore he placed a tally in a cave eighteen yards by twelve, which in time became full.

Later there was a son of an old worthy, called Fragrant Collection, who came to pay respects to the Master, with the aspiration to ask permission to leave the home life. The Master questioned him, 'Is it your body which leaves the home life, or your heart which leaves the home life?'

'I have come to leave the home life. It is neither body nor heart,' said Fragrant Collection.

'Since it is neither body nor heart,' said the master, 'who then leaves the home life?'

---

[155] The Buddha, the Dharma and the Sangha.

'A homeless one's self is without selfishness and because it is a selfless self his heart is not subject to birth and death. The heart not being subject to birth and death, this is the everlasting Way. All the Buddhas are also everlasting and the heart, without form or essence, is also like this.'

The master said, 'You should have a great awakening by which the heart will understand of itself. It is fitting to connect such a lofty spiritual seed so that it is in accord with the Buddha, the Dharma and the Sangha.' The master then shaved his head and as a monk he was administered the full precepts. Still addressing him the Master said, 'Before you were born your father dreamt of a golden sun. Your name shall be "Dhritaka".' He continued, 'The Tathāgata transmitted the Treasury of the Great Dharma-eye from one to another until it came to me. I now in turn pass it to you. Listen to my *gatha*:'

Heart is Heart from the very beginning
Yet the Original Heart is not an existent dharma.
Where Dharma is, there is Original Heart
Yet it is neither a heart nor an original dharma.

Having transmitted the Dharma he jumped into the air, showed the eighteen transformations, then took his original seat again, crossed his legs and passed away.

Dhritaka, using the bamboo tallies from the cave, cremated his body. He collected the *śarīra* relics and built a *stupa* for homage.

This took place in the thirtieth year of King Ping, corresponding to the thirty-seventh year of the sexagenarian cycle.

1.12   Dhritaka, the Fifth Patriarch

Dhritaka, the fifth patriarch, was a native of Magadha. Before his birth his father dreamt of a golden sun rising from his own house, illuminating heaven and earth, and in front [of the house] was a huge mountain all bedecked with jewels. At the peak of the mountain arose a spring gushing forth torrents in all directions.

Later [Dhritaka] happened upon Upagupta, who explained to him, 'The precious mountain refers to my body, the streaming torrents are the Dharma which is never exhausted. The sun rising from the house is you, just now entering into the Way. Illuminating heaven and earth is your wisdom gone beyond.'

The Master's original name was Fragrant Collection but now the teacher changed it to the Buddhist name Dhritaka, which means True Capacity.

Having heard his teacher's pronouncement Dhritaka was happy and joyful. He sang,

Very lofty is the seven-jewelled mountain
Forever spouting forth wisdom's spring
Changed into the taste of the True Dharma
It can save all who have a taste for it.

Then Master Upagupta also responded with a *gatha*:

I transmit the Dharma to you
It behoves you to show the Great Wisdom;
Let the golden sun rising from the house
Illumine Heaven and Earth.

When Dhritaka heard this wonderful *gatha* from his teacher, he humbly set himself to uphold it.

Later he went to Central India. In that kingdom there were eight thousand great recluses, the head of whom was Michaka. Hearing of the Master's arrival, he paid him a courtesy visit at the head of his assembly. He asked the Master, 'In ancient times, in the *Brahma* Heaven, we were of equal rank. Then I came across Ashita the recluse, who imparted to me his teachings. But you, O Master, became a disciple of the One with the ten powers, and you practiced Chan [meditation], with the result that our ways already parted six *kalpas* ago!'

The master replied, 'Disunited indeed through wearisome *kalpas*, though really not in vain! Now could be the time to abandon the crooked way and return to the true one by entering the Buddha Vehicle.'

Michaka said, 'Formerly Ashita the hermit gave me a prediction which said, "Now when you come across a fellow student from six *kalpas* ago, then you shall obtain the fruit that is without outflows". That we meet again now, is it not through our relationship from previous lives? Would that the Master's compassion facilitate my liberation!' So the Master ordained the sage and administered the precepts to him. The rest of the hermits maintained a haughty attitude at first, but the Master showed great spiritual penetration, so that all aspired to the heart of *Bodhi* and were ordained together.

Then the Master said to Michaka, 'In days gone by the Tathāgata privately transmitted the Treasury of the Great Dharma-eye to Mahākāśyapā. It has been transmitted from one master to another until it came to me. I now transmit it to you. You should cherish it.' Then he recited the following *gatha*:

Penetrating the Dharma of the Original Heart
There is neither Dharma nor no-dharma
Awakened is the same as not yet awakened
For there is neither Heart nor Dharma.

Having recited the *gatha*, the Master leapt into the air, showed the eighteen transformations and self-cremated through the fire-ray samādhi. Michaka and the eight thousand monks collected the *śarīra* relics and erected a *stupa* in the Pansa Mountains for their homage. This was in the fifth year of King Zhuang, corresponding to the twenty-sixth year of the sexagenarian cycle.

1.13   Michaka, the Sixth Patriarch

Michaka, the sixth patriarch, was a native of Central India. After receiving the transmission of the Dharma he travelled about until he came to a kingdom in Northern India. There he saw an auspicious golden cloud above the embrasure in the parapet of a walled town. Sighing in wonder he said, 'This is the emanation of a man of the Way; it must be that of a great being who will succeed me in the Dharma.' Then he entered the city and in the market place there was a man holding a wine-pitcher upside-down. The man asked, 'Where does the Master come from and where does he wish to go?'

'I come from my own heart and there is no place I wish to go,' replied the Master.

'Do you know what is in my hand?' asked the man.

'The pitcher you are handling has lost its purity,' responded the Master.

'Am I still not recognised by the master?' asked the man.

'"I" is not recognised. Recognised is the absence of "I",' said the Master, adding, 'examine your family name, afterwards I will show you the karmic connections.'

This man then recited a *gatha* by way of reply:

I, from innumerable *kalpas* until born in this country
Have had the family name Paradha,
Personal name Vasumitra.

Whereupon the Master said, 'My teacher Dhritaka said that when the World-Honoured One was once travelling about in Northern India he had said to Ānanda, "three hundred years after my death, in this country, there will be a wise man with the family name of Paradha and the personal name of Vasumitra who will be the seventh patriarch of Chan." The World-Honoured One knew of you and your wish to leave the home life.'

The man then put down the pitcher and made obeisance to the Master. Standing at his side, he said, 'I remember that in a distant *kalpa* I had made an offering of sandalwood and presented the Tathāgata with a precious throne-seat. Then that Buddha made a prediction concerning me, saying, "In the Auspicious Kalpa you will propagate the supreme teaching of Shakyamuni." This tallies with what the Master has said today. Please help me to emancipation.'

The Master then shaved his head, gave him the complete precepts and said to him, 'I now transmit to you the Treasury of the Eye of the True Dharma. Do not allow it to perish.' Then he recited a *gatha*:

There is no Heart, nothing to be obtained
Talk of obtained cannot be called Dharma.
Understanding Heart as no-Heart
Is to begin to understand
The Heart of the Heart-Dharma.

Having recited this *gatha*, the Master entered the speedy rousing of the lion samādhi, leapt into the air to the height of seven palm trees, then returned to his seat and cremated himself. Vasumitra collected the sacred bones, placed them in a case with seven jewels and then put this in the apex of a *stupa* that he had erected. This was in the fourteenth year of the reign of King Xiang, corresponding to the twenty-first year of the sexagenarian cycle.

1.14 Vasumitra, the Seventh Patriarch [156]

Vasumitra, the seventh patriarch, was from a kingdom in Northern India. The family name was Paradha. He always wore clean clothes and, carrying a wine-pitcher, would walk to the gate of the walled city either singing or whistling. People said he was mad. Upon coming across Michaka and the Master's relating of the Tathāgata's prediction, he remembered and understood the previous causal linkages. He relinquished his pitcher, left the home life and received the transmission of the Dharma.

Journeying to the country of Kamala his Buddhist activities flourished far and wide. Suddenly one day a sage appeared in front of his seat who said, 'My name is Buddhanandi and now I would like to engage in discussion with the Master.'

The Master said, 'Kind Sir! Discussion misses the meaning and the meaning cannot be discussed. If you intend to discuss meanings then in the end the discussion has no meaning!'

Buddhanandi knew then that the Master's case was superior and his heart submitted respectfully. He said, 'I wish to seek for the way, to benefit from the sweet nectar.' Then the Venerable Master shaved his head, administered the full precepts to him saying, 'The Treasury of the Tathāgata's True Dharma-eye I now transmit to you. You should guard and cherish it,' after which he recited the following *gatha*:

The Heart is like the realm of empty space
Revealing the equality of empty dharmas
When emptiness is experienced
There are no dharmas, neither good nor bad.

Then the Master entered the samādhi of the compassionate heart. *Brahman*, together with a heavenly host, came to pay their respects and to recite a *gatha* at this time:

---

[156] Probably not the same person as the follower of the Sarvastivāda school during the reign of King Kaniśka – a famous patron of Buddhism in India (regn. 15 BCE – 45 CE?). Vasumitra was the supposed author of many *Abhidharma* works. HIB: 275, Par. 302; HCB: 196; DCBT: 122b; BCA: 37-40.

All the sagely patriarchs of this auspicious *kalpa*
Work through the seventh one!
Oh Venerable One, please have a compassionate thought
And describe for us the Buddha-land!

So the Master arose from his samādhi and addressing the assembly said, 'The Dharma which I came to has no existent cause. Realisation of the Buddha-land is beyond existent or non-existent causes.' Having said this he entered samādhi once more and revealed his nirvāṇa. Buddhanandi buried his whole body in a seven-jewelled *stupa* that he erected on the site of the Master's original seat. This was in the seventeenth year of the reign of King Ding, corresponding to the eighth year of the sexagenarian cycle.

1.15 Buddhanandi, the Eighth Patriarch

The eighth patriarch, Buddhanandi, was a native of the kingdom of Kamala whose family name was Gotama. He had the protuberance on top of his head and his eloquence knew no obstructions. At the first meeting with Vasumitra he left the home life and received the teachings.

Later [Buddhanandi] went with his disciples on a missionary tour. Arriving in the kingdom of Vaishali he saw a white light rising above the house of a merchant in the city. He said to his followers, 'There must be a sage in this house, one who has not yet spoken a word, a true vessel of the Dharma who doesn't walk the four by-ways yet knows all about the pollutants.' As he finished speaking an old man came out of the house, and offering respectful greetings asked, 'Is there any help needed?'

'I am in search of an attendant,' replied the Master.

'I have a son named Buddhamitra,' said the old man, 'although he is fifty years old he has never yet talked or walked with shoes on.'

'If it is as you say then he is truly my disciple,' and on the Master's seeing him, Buddhamitra instantly got up, bowed respectfully and recited a *gatha*:

My mother and father are not my family
Who then is my real family?
All the Buddhas are not my way
Who then is my real way?

The Master responded with an answering *gatha*:

You recite as one familiar with the heart
Father and mother don't come into it.
Your actions accord with the Way
The Hearts of all the Buddhas are thus.
Searching outside there seem to be Buddhas
But for you it is not about indications;
If you wish to realise the Original Heart
It is neither close nor far away.

On hearing this wonderful *gatha*, Buddhamitra walked seven steps.

The Master said, 'This boy once came across a Buddha, as a result of which a great compassion arose in him to save all sentient beings, but he worried about the difficulties of abandoning the affections of his father and mother, so he just kept silent and stayed at home.'

The old man then allowed him to leave the home life, whereupon the Master administered the full precepts to him and said, 'I now entrust you with the Treasury of the True Dharma-eye of the Tathāgata. Do not let it perish.' Then he recited a *gatha*:

Emptiness is without inside or outside
The Heart of the Dharma is also like this.
If emptiness is understood
This penetrates the principle of true Suchness.

Buddhamitra, inheriting the Master's transmission, praised it with a *gatha*:

Our Master, one of the Chan patriarchs
Works through to obtain the eighth [generation]
The Dharma transforms people without number
May all beings come to awakening!

The Master Buddhanandi then showed his spiritual transformations and, resuming his original seat, entered cessation with great dignity. All the followers set up a jewelled *stupa* in which his entire body was buried. This was in the tenth year of the reign of King Jing, corresponding to the third year of the sexagenarian cycle.

1.16 Buddhamitra, the Ninth Patriarch

The ninth patriarch, Buddhamitra, was a native of Dhataka whose family came from the merchant class. Having received the care of the Buddha's transmission from Buddhanandi, he went on a missionary tour to Central India. At that time there was an elder called Incense Cover who came to visit, bringing a son with him. Greeting the Master respectfully, he said, 'This son was in the womb for sixty years, thus his name Difficult Birth. And once I came across a hermit who said that this boy was no ordinary one and might be a vessel of the Dharma. Today we have come across the Master – may the boy now leave the home life!' The Master then shaved his head and administered the precepts.

During the ceremony of ordination an auspicious light illuminated [the son's] seat and he felt the presence of thirty-seven holy relics, so he tirelessly applied himself all the more. Later, the Master said to him, 'The Treasury of the Great Dharma-eye of the Tathāgata I now give to you. You should cherish it.' Then he recited a *gatha*:

> The True Principle originally has no name
> Yet words can clarify the True Principle.
> On coming to the True Real Dharma
> It is neither a true, nor a false one.

The Master, having transmitted the Dharma, entered the samādhi of cessation, nirvāṇa. The followers cremated his physical body with incense, oil and sandalwood. They collected the *śarīra* relics and built a *stupa* for them at the Nālandā Monastery. This was in the thirty-third year of King Jing, corresponding to the fifty-first year of the sexagenarian cycle.

1.17 Parsva, the Tenth Patriarch

The tenth patriarch, Parsva, was from Central India. His original name was Difficult Birth. When Parsva was about to be born, his father had a dream of a white elephant on whose back was a jewelled seat. On top of that seat was a bright pearl. From open gates rays of light were illuminating the four assemblies. Then he woke up and the baby was born.

Afterwards, Parsva met master Buddhamitra, who took him as personal attendant. He had never lain down to sleep so his name was the Venerable Xie – 'the flank not reaching the couch'. His first [missionary tour] was to the kingdom of Pataliputra.

Once, resting under a tree, he pointed to the ground with his right hand and said to his followers, 'When this ground changes to the colour of gold then a sage will enter our assembly.' Having said this the ground changed to the colour of gold and the son of a wealthy dignitary, Punyayasas was there, palms joined respectfully, standing in front of Master [Parsva], who said, 'Where have you come from?'

'My heart does not travel,' said Punyayasas.

'Where do you live?' asked the Master.

'My heart abides nowhere,' replied the younger.

'Are you unattached?' asked the Master.

'All the Buddhas are like this too,' replied the younger.

'You are not all the Buddhas,' said the Master.

'All the Buddhas are also not the Master,' replied he.

So the Master recited a *gatha*:

By this ground changing to the colour of gold
I knew already that a sage would come.
He will sit under the Bodhi-tree
And the flower of awakening will be born.

Punyayasas responded with a *gatha*:

The Master sits on gold-coloured ground
Forever teaching the true realisation
Turning the light to shine on me
He allows entry into samādhi.

The Master, seeing the boy's wish, ordained him into the homeless life, gave him the complete precepts and said to him, 'The Treasury of the Tathāgata's Great Dharma-eye I now hand over to you; guard and cherish it.' Then he recited a *gatha*:

The true essence is naturally true
Being true it is said to have principle;
Real understanding of this is the True Dharma.
There is no going, also no abiding.

Having transmitted the Dharma, the Master then manifested spiritual transformation, entered nirvāṇa and created the fire for self-cremation. The four
assemblies built *stupas* all around and placing their pieces of cloth containing
the *śarīra* relics within them and paid them homage.

This was in the twentieth year of King Cheng, corresponding to the thirty-
sixth year of the sexagenarian cycle.

1.18 Punyayasas, the Eleventh Patriarch

The eleventh patriarch, Punyayasas, was a native of the kingdom of Pataliputra,
whose family name was Gotama. His father's name was Precious Body.

After receiving the Dharma from Master Parsva he went in search to the
kingdom of Baranasi. There the Mahāsattva Aśvaghoṣa[157] welcomed him with
every courtesy and proceeded to question him.

'I would like to know the Buddha,' asked Aśvaghoṣa, 'what is he?'

'You wish to know the Buddha,' replied Master Punyayasas, 'it is that
which does not know.'

'Since Buddha is unknowable,' countered Aśvaghoṣa, 'how to know that then?'

'Since Buddha is unknowable, how to know that it is not that either?'
replied the Master.

'This is the principle of the saw cutting things down,' said Aśvaghoṣa.

'No,' said the Master, 'it is the principle of the tree.'

'But what is the principle of the saw cutting?' asked Aśvaghoṣa.

'To come out equally with the teacher,' replied the Master.

'And what is the principle of the tree?'

'That you come to my understanding,' said the Master.

Aśvaghoṣa immediately had a great awakening. He prostrated himself, wishing
to be ordained and have his head shaved.

---

[157] A great Sanskrit poet, dramatist and devout Buddhist, author of the famous *Buddha-
carita* (Acts of the Buddha). IB: 133ff; HIB: 591, par. 655.

Master Punyayasas then told the assembly, 'This great warrior was the ruler of the Vaishali kingdom in times past. His country had a tribe of warriors who went as naked as their horses, so the King, making use of his spiritual power, divided his body up so as to become silk worms, to make clothes [for his men]. But the warriors cried mournfully, moved to affection by their loss. Later the king was reborn in Central India where he was called Aśvaghoṣa, which means Horse Cry.'

The Tathāgata had previously also made a prediction by saying, 'Six hundred years after my decease there will be a sage – Aśvaghoṣa – who, in the kingdom of Baranasi, will crush heretical ways by leading countless numbers of people to the other shore, following my transmission of the teachings.'

'Verily, the time has now come,' said Punyayasas and told him, 'the Treasury of the Great Dharma-eye of the Tathāgata I now pass on to you.' Then he recited a *gatha*:

Delusion and awakening are like darkness and light
Light and dark are not mutually exclusive
Now, handing over the Dharma of darkness and light
It is neither one nor is it two.

After the Master had transmitted this Dharma he went into spiritual transformation and then, fresh and cool, entered complete cessation.

The assembly erected a jewelled *stupa* in which they interred his entire body. This was in the nineteenth year of the reign of King An, corresponding to the thirty-fifth year of the sexagenarian cycle.

1.19 Aśvaghoṣa, the Twelfth Patriarch.

The twelfth patriarch, Aśvaghoṣa Mahāsattva,[158] was a native of the kingdom of Baranasi. He was also called Surpassing Merit because all that he did or did not do was of the most outstanding merit. After receiving the Dharma from Master Punyayasas he went to Pataliputra to turn the wonderful Wheel of the Dharma.

Suddenly there appeared an old man in front of his seat one day, prostrating to the ground. The Master (Aśvaghoṣa) said to the assembly, 'This is not a common man. Strange things could happen.' As soon as he had said this,

---

[158] Mahāsattva, 'great being', is a standard epithet for senior bodhisattvas.

the old man became invisible whilst a gold-coloured man sprang up from the ground, transforming into a woman. Pointing with her right hand at the Master she recited a *gatha*:

All praise to the Venerable Elder.
Having received the Tathāgata's prediction
The penetration of the prime meaning
Is proclaimed here today.

Having finished the recitation she became invisible in the blink of an eye.

'A demon will come to contend with me for power,' said the Master, and at once a violent storm arose, darkening heaven and earth. 'This is the sign that the demon is coming,' said Aśvaghoṣa, 'I must despatch him.' Pointing up into the sky, he caused to appear an enormous golden dragon, which emitted an awesome spiritual power. The lofty mountains trembled, but the Master sat down on his seat in a dignified manner, whilst the demonic events died away.

Seven days later there was a small insect, very much like a moth, hiding itself under the seat of the Master who, taking it in his hand, showed it to the assembly, saying, 'This is the very same demon, changed in form, just eaves-dropping on our Dharma-talk.' Then he put it down to let it free, but the demon couldn't move. The Master said to it, 'If you only take refuge in the Three Jewels then you will obtain spiritual transformation', whereupon the demon assumed his original form, made obeisance and repented.

'What is your name and how many are your dependants?' asked the Master.

'My name is Kapimala and there are three thousand dependents,' replied the demon.

'You have exhausted your spiritual power,' said the Master, 'now what transformations are left?'

'I can change the great ocean into a tiny drop,' he answered.

'But can you change the Innate Ocean Nature?' asked the Master.

'What is the Innate Ocean Nature? I have never heard of such a thing!' said the demon.

The Master then talked of the Ocean of the Innate Nature, saying, 'Mountains, rivers and the great earth arise on its dependence, just as samādhi and the Six Spiritual Penetrations come forth from it.'[159]

---

[159] The six spiritual penetrations (*Ṣaḍabhijñā*) of Buddhas: the heavenly ear, heavenly

When Kapimala heard this, faith arose in his heart. He beseeched ordination for himself and for his three thousand followers, so the Master summoned five hundred *Arhats* to administer the complete precepts to them.

Master Aśvaghoṣa said to him, 'The Treasury of the Great Dharma-eye of the Tathāgata I now pass on to you, listen to my *gatha:*'

Hidden and revealed is the Great Dharma
Awakening and ignorance are originally not-two.
Now, passing on the awakened understanding of the Dharma
It is not something to take or leave.

After the Dharma was transmitted [the Master] entered the samādhi of the swift dragon-force, projected his body into the air in the form of a sun-disc and promptly revealed his extinction.

The four assemblies placed his real body in the Dragon Shrine.

This was in the forty-second year of the reign of King Xian, corresponding to the thirty-first year of the sexagenarian cycle.

1.20 Kapimala, the Thirteenth Patriarch

The thirteenth patriarch, Kapimala, was a native of the kingdom of Pataliputra. At first he was a heretic with three thousand followers who understood all the heterodox theories. After obtaining the Dharma from Master Aśvaghoṣa he lead his supporters to Western India, where there was a crown prince by the name of Free-as-Clouds who welcomed the renowned Master and invited him to the palace in order to pay him due respect. The Master said to the crown prince, 'The Tathāgata had a teaching that monks may not be intimate with powerful ministers and their sovereign when entering their country.'

The crown prince answered, 'To the north of our city there is a great mountain and in that mountain there is a stone cave. Would the Master like to practice meditation there then?'

The Master answered in the affirmative and went. After walking several *li* up into the mountain he encountered a huge serpent, but kept to his way without

eye, knowledge of the thoughts of others, knowledge of the previous lives of self and others, the power to be anywhere or do anything at will, knowledge of the way to the exhaustion of the passions. See DCBT. 123a; 138b.

looking round at it. The serpent then coiled itself around the Master's body, so he recited the Three Refuges and the serpent, having heard them, departed. The Master then reached the stone cave, from which an old man, dressed in white and palms together in greeting, came out and enquired after him.

'Where do you live?' asked the Master.

'In former times I was a monk greatly enjoying tranquillity,' answered the old man, 'but there were novice monks who came asking more and more questions until I became annoyed at having to answer, so that a feeling of hatred arose. At the end of that life I fell into a serpent's body and have been living in this stone cave for one thousand years. Fortunately coming across the Master just now I obtained a hearing of the Dharma-precepts and so come to thank you.'

The Master asked, 'Does this mountain have others living here?'

'If you go north for ten *li* there is a great tree which shelters five hundred large dragons. The king of the tree is called Nāgārjuna (Long Shu, 'tree-dragon'); he often gives Dharma-talks to the dragon assembly. I also go to listen.'

The Master then went with his assembly of followers to this place. Nāgārjuna came out and greeted the Master saying, 'Deep in these mountains, in solitary peace, dragon-pythons have their abode. Why does the most honoured one of great virtue waste his spiritual energy [in coming here]?'

'It is not I who is the most honoured one,' was the Master's reply, 'I come to visit a wise man.'

Nāgārjuna thought to himself, 'Has this Master obtained the root propensities[160] and the clear eye of the Way or not? And does this great sage then continue in the True Vehicle?'

'Although you haven't expressed it, I already know your wish,' said the Master. 'You are only interested in being ordained a Buddhist monk, so why bother yourself about whether I am a sage or not?'

Having heard this Nāgārjuna repented humbly and the Master liberated him and gave the full precepts to all the assembly of five hundred dragons.

---

[160] The five kinds of Root Nature – study of the void Root Nature, which corrects all illusions of time and space; the ability to differentiate all the natures of phenomena Root Nature, which transforms the living; the middle way Root Nature, which attains insight into Buddha's Laws; the sage Root Nature, which produces sagehood by destroying ignorance and the Bodhi-rank Root Nature which produces Buddhahood – these were classified by the Faxiang school, see DCBT.124a.

Again the Master spoke to Nāgārjuna saying, 'Now I pass on to you the Treasury of the Tathāgata's Great Dharma-eye. Listen clearly to this *gatha*:'

Neither a concealed nor a revealed Dharma
It expounds the region of True Reality.
Awakened to this Dharma concealed and revealed
It is neither foolish nor wise.

Having transmitted this Dharma [Master Kapimala] showed the spiritual transformations and created fire for the cremation of his body. Nāgārjuna collected five-coloured *sarīra* relics and erected a *stupa* in which to bury them.

This was in the forty-sixth year of the reign of King Nan, corresponding to the twenty-ninth year of the sexagenarian cycle.

1.21 Nāgārjuna, the Fourteenth Patriarch

The fourteenth patriarch, Master Nāgārjuna (tree-dragon),[161] also called Dragon Conqueror, was a native of Western India who obtained the Dharma from Master Kapimala at their very first meeting. Later he went to Southern India where many people in that part of the country had faith in the efficacy of good works. When they heard Master [Nāgārjuna] expounding the wonderful Dharma they said to one another, 'The first thing in life is for a man to have fortunate *karma*. Followers talk about the Buddha-nature, but who can see it?'

The Master said to them, 'If you wish to see the Buddha-nature then first get rid of your lassitude.'

One of them asked, 'Is the Buddha-nature large or small?'

'Neither large nor small,' replied the Master, 'neither broad nor narrow, without good fortune or retribution; it is not born and does not die.'

Those who heard of a principle so superior all returned to their beginners' resolve. Then the Master returned to his seat and showed them his being, free of delusion. It was like the disc of the full moon. The whole assembly could only hear the sound of the Dharma but could see no sign of the Master. Amongst the

---

[161] Nāgārjuna is one of the greatest Buddhist Masters of all time. As an ascetic he is said to have lived under the shade of an Arjuna tree (*Pentaptera Arjuna*, sacred Indian tree); *Nāga* is Pali/Sanskrit for 'serpent' or 'snake'. Nāgārjuna is sometimes identified with the Buddhist sage Aravana Adigal of southern India.

assembly was the son of an old venerable by the name of Kanadeva. He asked the others, 'Do you know the meaning of this form or not?'

The assembly answered, 'It has never been seen so how is it possible to know what it is?'

Kanadeva said, 'What is being demonstrated to us is the Master's showing of the essence and form of the Buddha-nature. How is it possible to know that? By the form of the formless samādhi which is like the full moon. The knowledge of the Buddha-nature is vast and clear!'

Having said this, the moon disc disappeared and the Master, returned to his original seat, and recited a *gatha*:

> With my revealing the form of the full moon
> The essence of all the Buddhas is expressed
> The expounding of the Dharma is not its form
> Even by discernment it has no sound or shape.

On hearing this *gatha* the assembly suddenly awakened to the Unborn and all wished to leave the home life to seek for emancipation. The Master then shaved their heads and instructed the sages to give them the precepts.

The country had for a long time more than five thousand heretics who were practising the advanced magic arts, and they were admired and respected by all in the assembly. The Master converted them all, having them take refuge in the Three Jewels.

The Master [Nāgārjuna] also gave to the world the *Mahā-Prajñāpāramitā-Śāstra,* the *Madhyamika Śāstra,* and the *Dvādaśanikāya Śāstra,* all of which he authored.[162]

Later he said to his most senior disciple Kanadeva, 'The Treasury of the True Dharma-eye I now pass on to you. Listen to my *gatha*:'

---

[162] The Three Śāstra School, (Chinese, Sanlun) based its tenets on the *Madhyamika Śāstra* (Treatise on the Middle Way) and the *Dvādaśanikāya Śāstra,* (Treatise on the Twelve Gates), both authored by Nāgārjuna and the *Sata Śāstra* (The One Hundred Verses Treatise) by Āryadeva. These three Śāstras were translated by Kumārajīva, T. 1564; T. 1568; T. 1569 respectively. They are said to disperse the Eight Misleading Ideas (birth, death, end, permanence and identity, difference, coming, and going) and establish the interpenetration of the relative and absolute.

To clarify the Dharma, concealed and revealed,
Just the principle of liberation is spoken of
But if the Heart does not get caught up in Dharma
Then neither joy nor anger exists.

Having finished the transmission of the Dharma the Master entered the full moon samādhi and freely showed his spiritual transformations. Then, resuming his original seat, collected, he entered cessation. Kanadeva and the four assemblies together built a jewelled *stupa* in which to bury him,

This was in the thirty-fifth year of the reign of Qinshi Huangdi, corresponding to the twenty-sixth year of the sexagenarian cycle.

End of Book One

Book Two

2.22 Kanadeva, the Fifteenth Patriarch

The fifteenth patriarch, Kanadeva, came from a kingdom in Southern India. His family name was Vesala. At first he sought good fortune but also took pleasure in debate. Later he had an interview with Great Teacher Nāgārjuna, under whom he would attain the entrance.

Nāgārjuna knew that this was a man of wisdom, so he first sent an attendant [to Kanadeva] with a full bowl of water, which was placed in front of his seat. The Venerable [Kanadeva] looked at it, then took a needle and dropped it into the water; it sank. Happily he was in accord with the deep meaning of Nāgārjuna, who then expounded the Dharma by showing him the outward characteristic of the 'full moon contemplation' without leaving his seat.[163] Only his voice could be heard, his form could not be seen. The Venerable [Kanadeva] said to the assembly, 'Today with this auspicious event the Teacher is revealing the Buddha-nature, demonstrating a teaching without sound or form.'

After obtaining the Dharma the master [Kanadeva] went to the kingdom of Vīrasana. A virtuous elder by the name of Brahman Virtue lived there and one day in his garden there arose a great fungus-like mushroom. It tasted delicious but only the elder and his second son Rahulata were capable of picking and eating it. Every time they picked it there grew another in its place, but the rest of the family couldn't even see it. The Master knew the antecedent cause and on visiting the family Virtuous Elder asked him about it. The Master said, 'In days long gone your family had supported a monk whose Spiritual Eye was not yet clear so that the alms given to him in good faith were of no benefit. He is making amends now by being a great mushroom; only you and your son, who were sincere in giving support, can obtain the enjoyment of it, whilst the rest of the family cannot.'

'What is your age?' asked the Master.

'Seventy-nine,' answered the Elder.

The Master then recited the following *gatha*:

Entering the Way without penetrating principle
Is to repeatedly give one's own body as alms
When you reach eighty-one
The mushroom will no longer grow on this tree.

---

[163] For the outward appearance of the 'moon-disc contemplation' and its application to the development of *Bodhi* within, see DCBT: 157a.

On hearing this *gatha* the Elder's admiration and respect increased. He said, 'Your disciple is old and in failing health, so it is not possible to serve the Master, but please allow me to relinquish this son to follow the Master into the homeless life!'

'In days long gone,' said the Master, 'the Tathāgata had made a prediction that this son would, in the second five-hundred year period, be a great master of the teaching. Today's encounter is in accord with that antecedent cause.' Then the Master shaved [the son's] head and took him as his attendant.

Arriving in Pataliputra the Master and his followers heard that many heretics wished to separate from the Buddha-dharma and had already been scheming to do this for a long time. The Master, holding a long banner-flag, went into their midst. 'Why don't you pass on?' asked one of them.

'Why don't you retreat?' came the Master's reply.

'You seem to be a mean person,' said the heretic.

'You seem to be a fine fellow!' answered the Master.

'Which Dharma do you comprehend?'

'You have not comprehended any!' countered the Master.

'I wish to attain Buddhahood', said the heretic.

'I have already attained Buddhahood,' said the Master.

'You are not equal to attaining it!' replied the heretic.

'Factually it has to be said that I have attained and that it is really you who have not attained,' said the Master.

'Since you cannot have attained why talk of attainment?' asked the heretic.

'Because you have the "I",' said the Master, 'therefore it is not attained. Because I am without the "I", I have naturally attained it.'

This exchange had already humbled the heretics and they asked the Master's name.

'I am called Kanadeva,' said the Master. Having already got wind of the Master's fame they repented and apologised. At the same time there were still difficult points being asked backwards and forwards but the Master cut through them all with unhindered eloquence. Because of this they submitted to ordination. Then the Master told his most senior disciple, Rahulata, of the transmission of the Dharma-eye, with a *gatha*:

To the person actually receiving Dharma-transmission
It is spoken of as the principle of emancipation
Yet in the Dharma there is really nothing to testify to
For it is without beginning and without end.

The Master having recited the *gatha* entered the arousing of the swift [lion] samādhi; his body emitted eight rays and then he returned to the peace of cessation.

His disciples erected a *stupa* in which to pay him homage. This was in the nineteenth year of the reign of Emperor Wendi, in the Former Han Dynasty, corresponding to the seventeenth year of the sexagenarian cycle.

2.23 **Rahulata,** the Sixteenth Patriarch

The sixteenth patriarch, Rahulata, was a native of the Kapila kingdom. He came to Śrāvastī city on a missionary tour, where there was a river called Golden Waters, of taste exceedingly sweet whose stream constantly reflected the forms of five Buddhas. The Master said to the assembly, 'At the source of this river, some five hundred *li* upstream, there is a sage, Sanghanandi, who lives in that place. The Buddha had recorded that a thousand years after him this sage would continue the calling of a Wise One.'

After saying this he led all his students upstream to visit there and when they arrived, saw Sanghanandi sitting quietly in meditation. The Master and assembly looked on at him but it was only after twenty-one days that he emerged from meditation.

The Master then asked him, 'Was your body in meditation or was your heart in meditation?'

'Both body and heart was in meditation,' replied Sanghanandi.

'If body and heart are both in meditation, what is it that comes out of it or goes into it?' asked the Master.

'Although there is coming out and going in,' replied Sanghanandi, 'there is no loss of the form of meditation. Like a bucket in a well, the substance of the bucket is stable.'

'If the [substance] of the bucket is always the same, whether in the well or out of the well, what is it that comes out and goes in?' asked the Master.

'You wish to say that the bucket changes,' answered Sanghanandi, 'and then ask "what is going in and out?" Then you talk of the bucket going in and out – but the bucket doesn't change.'

'If the bucket is in the well,' asked Master Rahulata , 'what comes out? If the bucket is out, what is left in the well?'

'If the bucket is out of the well,' said Sanghanandi, 'that which is left is not the bucket. If the bucket is in the well, nothing comes out.'

'This is not the meaning,' said the Master [Rahulata].

'Your point is not clear,' countered Sanghanandi.

'Your understanding could be faulty,' said the Master.

'And your interpretation is not complete,' said Sanghanandi

'Yours is the incomplete one, mine the truly complete,' said the Master.

'My understanding is surely complete, because it is not a personal one,' said Sanghanandi.

'My understanding has already been completed as "I is no-I",' replied the Master.

'Again, what is the interpretation of "I is no-I"?'

'If "I is no-I", then your understanding is complete,' said the Master.

'Oh kind Master!' asked Sanghanandi, 'From which sage did you obtain this "no-I"?'

'My master Kanadeva certified this "no-I",' said the Master.

'Homage to Master Kanadeva who produced the Kind Sir!,' said Sanghanandi, 'because of the Kind Sir's "no-I", I would like him to be my teacher!'

'I have already become "no-I", so it is you who must realise this "I" [of no-I] for yourself. If the teacher is going to be me, know that this me is not a personal "I",' said the Master.

Sanghanandi's heart's wish suddenly became clear to him and he begged for liberation. 'Your heart is free,' said the Master, 'it is no longer the personal "I" which binds you.' Having said this he took a golden bowl in his right hand and ascended to the Brahma Palace to fetch food and incense in order to feed the large assembly, but they immediately engendered a dislike for it in their hearts. 'It is not my fault,' said he, 'it is your own *karma*' and so he let Sanghanandi share his own seat and eat of the same food. The Assembly responded with surprise.

'The reason why you don't come to this food is due to this,' said the Master, 'you should know that the one sharing my seat is the Tathāgata King of the Sala Trees of a by-gone era, descended again out of compassion for all things. All of you too, in the Auspicious Kalpa, had already reached the stage of the three fruits[164], but had not yet experienced the absence of the outflows of the passions.'

'In our teacher's spiritual strength we can have faith,' said the assembly, 'as for the pronouncement that he is a Buddha from the past, this we have our private doubts about.'

---

[164] Stream Enterer, Once Returner and Non-Returner.

Sanghanandi knew that some haughtiness had arisen amongst the assembly, so he said, 'When the World-Honoured One was in the world the earth was even and flat. There were no hills or mounds and the water of the rivers and streams was beautiful and sweet to the taste, whilst grasses and trees flourished. The kingdom's soil was fertile and the eight sufferings[165] did not exist, only the practice of the Ten Noble Deeds.[166] From the twin trees, it has been more than eight hundred years since Buddha revealed his cessation and the world became a wasteland. The trees have withered and men are without unconditional faith: 'Right Vigilance'[167] is shallow, for men do not believe in Suchness and only love spiritual power.'

As he finished speaking [Sanghanandi] put his open right hand into the ground until he reached the diamond wheel sphere. Taking sweet dew water up with a porcelain vessel, he carried it to the gathering. Seeing this, the great assembly suddenly admired him, respectfully repented and made obeisance. Then Master Rahulata had Sanghanandi receive the Eye of the Dharma-transmission with a *gatha*:

In the Dharma truly nothing is to be witnessed
It cannot be grasped or laid aside
Dharma is not a form existent or non-existent.
Say, how could inside and outside arise then?

Having transmitted the Dharma he peacefully sat on his seat and went into quiescence.

The four assemblies built a *stupa*. This was in the twenty-eighth year of the reign of Emperor Wu of the Former Han dynasty, corresponding to the fifth year of the sexagenarian cycle.

2.24 Sanghanandi, the Seventeenth Patriarch

The seventeenth patriarch, Sanghanandi, was the son of King Precious Adornment of Śrāvastī city. From birth he could talk, always praising things to do

---

[165] The Eight Distresses: birth, age, sickness, death. Parting with what we love, meeting with what we hate, unattained aims, the ills of the five *skandhas*. See DCBT. 39b

[166] Ten Noble Deeds – non-committal of the Ten Sins. DCBT.47a

[167] Usually translated as 'Right Mindfulness', it is the seventh of the Eightfold Nobel Path.

with the Buddha. When he was seven years old he wearied of worldly pleasures and recited this *gatha* to his parents:

Homage to the great compassionate father
And to dear mother of flesh and bones
Today I wish to leave the home life –
Have compassion for such a hard decision!

His parents were determined to stop him, so he stopped eating. Then they allowed him to maintain the precepts whilst living at home, with the name of Sanghanandi. The monk Dhyanalita was assigned to be his teacher and for the next nineteen years he never slackened. But the Master always thought to himself, 'How can I leave the home life whilst living in the king's palace?' One evening a heavenly light shone down. Seeing an even road ahead and without waking up, he walked slowly for about ten *li*, until he was in front of a cave in the face of a great cliff and there he sat down quietly.

The father, since his son had gone, expelled Dhyanalita from his country and went in search of his son but his whereabouts remained unknown. Ten years past and the Master had by then inherited the Dharma and the prediction [of future Buddhahood].

He went on a mission-tour to the kingdom of Madra.[168] Suddenly one day there was a fresh breeze surrounding his assembly, extremely delightful and comforting, but nobody knew its source. The Master said, 'This is the wind of the Virtuous Dao. A sage should be appearing in the world to inherit the Lamp of the Patriarchs.' Having said this he used his spiritual power to help all of the great assembly to travel to a mountain valley. At mealtime they came to the foot of a peak. 'On top of this peak,' said the Master to his assembly, 'there is a purple cloud in the shape of a canopy. This is where the sage lives.' Then, after pacing up and down for quite some time together with the whole assembly, they saw, in a mountain hut, a young man holding a round mirror and coming straight towards the Master.

'How old are you?' inquired the Master.

'One hundred,' was the reply.

'But you are still young in years, why do you say one hundred?' asked the Master.

---

[168] The modern Punjab province of Pakistan.

'I do not understand the principle but truly it is one hundred years,' said he. 'Do you have the propensities for wisdom?' asked the Master.

'Buddha said that if a man becomes a hundred yet does not understand all the functions of the Buddha, then it is as if he is not yet one day old when it comes to clarifying them,' said the boy.

'What does that thing in your hand signify?' asked the Master.

'The Great Perfect Mirror of all the Buddhas is flawless both inside and outside,' said the boy, 'and two men see alike because all forms are the same to the Heart-Eye.'

The father and mother, on hearing their son thus, relinquished him and let him leave the home life. The Master then conducted him back to his native place and after administering the precepts, named him Gayasata.

Once, on hearing the sound of the wind blowing through the bronze temple bell, the Master asked Teacher Gayasata, 'Is the bell sounding or the wind sounding?'

'Neither the bell nor the wind,' replied Gayasata, 'only my heart is sounding.'

'Whose heart?' asked the Master.

'That by which all is quiescent and calm,' said Gayasata.

'Very good! Very good!' said the Master. 'Who but you will continue my Way!' Then he transmitted the Dharma with a *gatha*:

The heart-ground is originally birthless
The causal ground arises from relative causes
Relative cause and seed do not impede each other
The flower and fruit also respond thus.

The Master, having transmitted the Dharma and with his right hand holding on to the branch of a tree, went into transformation. The great assembly discussed the situation, saying, 'The Master returned to quiescence under the tree, thus he also transmitted a shelter to the following generation!' Then they tried to lift his entire body for burial in a *stupa* on a flat mountaintop but their combined strength could not lift it, so they built the *stupa* under the tree.

This was in the thirteenth year of the reign of the Emperor Zhao of the Former Han dynasty, corresponding to the forty-fourth year of the sexagenarian cycle.

2.25 Gayasata, the Eighteenth Patriarch

The eighteenth patriarch, Gayasata, was a native of the kingdom of Madra, whose family name was Udra Ramaputra. His father's name was Heavenly Parasol, his mother's All Wise. Having had a dream of a great Deva holding a mirror she became pregnant and fully seven days later she gave birth to Gayasata. The lustre of his body was smooth as porcelain and even before he had been washed the boy had a naturally pure fragrance.

When he was young the boy loved quietude and his speech was always pure. He roamed about holding a mirror. When he met Master Sanghanandi he obtained release.

Later he led his followers to the kingdom of Tukhāra. There over the house of a *Brahmin* family he sensed a strange atmosphere. The Master was just about to enter the house when the householder Kumorata came to the door and asked, 'Whose followers are you?'

'These are disciples of the Buddha,' said the Master.

The hearing of Buddha's name caused a sudden terror in the heart of Kumorata and he immediately shut the door. The Master himself knocked on the door for a good long while. Finally Kumorata shouted from inside, 'There's no one at home!'

'Who answers that there is no one?' called the Master.

When Kumorata heard these words he knew that this was no ordinary man so he spontaneously opened the door and welcomed him in.

'In a time long past,' said the Master, 'the World-Honoured One made a prediction saying, "one thousand years after my cessation a great being will appear in Tukhāra to pass on the wonderful transmission." Your meeting me today fulfils this most propitiously.' Thereupon there arose in Kumorata the wisdom that had accumulated for so long, so that he wished sincerely to submit to the monk's life. He received the precepts and the Dharma was transmitted to him with this *gatha*:

There is the seed and there is the heart-ground
Primary and secondary causes can bring forth the sprout
In the secondary cause there is no obstruction
It is born ever again yet is Unborn.

Having transmitted the Dharma the Master leapt into the air, displayed the eighteen spiritual transformations and changed into the Fire-ray Samādhi for the self cremation of his body. The assembly built a *stupa* for the *śarīra* relics.

This was in the twentieth year of the reign of Emperor Cheng of the Former Han dynasty, corresponding to the forty-fifth year of the sexagenarian cycle.

2.26 **Kumorata,** the Nineteenth Patriarch

The nineteenth patriarch, Kumorata, was the son of a *Brahmin* from the kingdom of Tukhāra. In the distant past he lived in the Independent Heaven, the sixth heaven of the realm of desire. Gazing at a bodhisattva's necklace of precious stones, there suddenly arose craving in his heart, so he fell down to birth in the Heaven of the Thirty-Three, the second heaven in the realm of desire.[169] There he heard Kaushika of the Kushikas[170]expounding on the *Prajñāpāramitā* and was overwhelmed by this Dharma, such that he ascended to the Brahma Heaven in the realm of form. Because of his root intelligence he skilfully expounded the essentials of the Dharma so that all the Heavenly Masters took him as their teacher.

When it came to the time of the patriarchal transmission he descended to Tukhāra. Later in life he went to Central India, where a great being by the name of Jāyatā said to him, 'At home, although my mother and father have pure faith in the Three Jewels, they have often been afflicted by sickness and all their undertakings have not come up to expectations, whilst my neighbour has for a long time been behaving like Chandala [the Outcast][171] and yet he is always bold and healthy and whatever he does turns out well. Why his good fortune and what is our crime?'

'Why so full of doubts?' replied the Master. 'The fruition of good and bad takes place in past, present and future. In general one regularly sees that the benevolent may die young and the violent live long; that the unfilial may have good luck, the righteous bad luck. They even talk of the disappearance of the cause and effect, of vice and good fortune being nonsense. They really don't know that effects follow the cause like a shadow, that even the slightest excess

---

[169] For details of Buddhist cosmology see Cheetham, E. *Fundamentals of Mainstream Buddhism*. London: Grove Edition, 1996

[170] Kaushika, of the family of Kushika, family name of Indra, ruler of the second realm of desire. DCTB: 188,b.

[171] A man of the lowest and most despised class; he bore a flag and sounded a bell to warn of his presence so as not to pollute others. Converts from this class were admitted for ordination into the Buddhist Sangha. DCTB: 326a.

errs, that even if a thousand million *kalpas* were to pass, still effects don't wear away or perish.'

When Jāyatā heard these words his doubts were suddenly dispelled. The Master continued, 'Although you have faith in the three *karmas*[172] there is still no clarity about *karma* being born of Illusion, that Illusion is due to the existence of Consciousness and that Consciousness depends on non-awakening and that non-awakening depends on Heart. The Heart is originally clean and pure, is without birth and death, without acts of creation, without retribution, without gain and loss, utterly quiescent and completely spiritual. If you enter this Dharma-gate you can be counted equal with all the Buddhas. All good and bad, selfish activity or selfless activity, all are like dreams and apparitions.'

Jāyatā received the sense of these words and there arose in him the accumulated wisdom of ages, so that he earnestly sought to leave the home life. Having received the complete precepts Master Kumorata said to him, 'The time for my peaceful end has come – you should continue propagating the Dharma-practice.' Then he transmitted the Eye of the Dharma with a *gatha*:

[The True] Nature is supreme, originally birthless;
As it is said to the one who seeks –
That since there is nothing to acquire in the Dharma,
Why cherish certainties one way or another?

The Master said, 'This was the poem the Tathāgata Wonderful Sound uttered on seeing the purity of the [True] Nature. You should transmit it to future students.' Having said this he seated himself and rent his own face with his fingernails so that it was like a lotus flower in bloom. A great light radiated, lighting up the four assemblies and then he entered tranquil cessation.

Jāyatā built a *stupa*, in the fourteenth year of the new dynasty, corresponding to the nineteenth year of the sexagenarian cycle.

2.27 Jāyatā, the Twentieth Patriarch

The twentieth patriarch, Jāyatā, was from a kingdom in Northern India. His wisdom and knowledge was deep and intelligent, his instruction and guidance beyond reckoning.

---

[172] The consequences of the acts of body, speech and mind.

In later years he went to the city of Rajagrha, where he expounded the sudden teaching. There were many scholars there who only valued debating. Their leader was Vasubandhu, which means Everywhere Active. He always took one meal a day, never lay down to sleep and prostrated to the Buddha six times daily. He was pure and without desire and respected by his followers.

The Master [Jāyatā] wished to liberate him, so he first asked [Vasubandhu's] followers, 'This "Everywhere Active" is disciplined and can practice pure living but is he able to attain the Buddha's Way?'

His followers answered, 'Our teacher really makes great efforts so why should he be unable to?'

'Your teacher is far from the Way,' said the Master, 'even supposing that he kept on practising for as many *kalpas* as there have been atoms in the universe so far, all is on a false foundation.'

'What meritorious practices has the Master accumulated that he jeers at our teacher?' responded his followers.

'I do not seek the Way, but neither do I go against it,' said the Master, 'I do not worship Buddha but neither am I haughty nor superficial. I do not sit long in meditation but neither am I negligent. I may not eat just once a day, yet do not over indulge. Even though I don't know what enough is, yet I am not greedy and in my heart there are no expectations. This is called the Way.'

When Vasubandhu had heard this he gave rise to the wisdom without outflows and joyfully praised the Master.

'Did you understand my words or not?' the Master asked the assembly once more. 'The reason for my acting like this was on account of his heart's urge to search the Way. He is [like] a string on a musical instrument, too tense and it breaks. Therefore I didn't praise him by letting him settle in an easy place, but had him enter the Wisdom of all the Buddhas.'

'I just curbed you, in front of your followers,' continued the Master to "Everywhere Active", 'did you attain to the state of not fretting about that in your heart of hearts?'

'I remember being born in the realm Ever Calm and Happy[173] ten *kalpas* ago,' replied Vasubandhu, 'where the master of Wisdom was Pure Moon, who predicted that I would experience the fruit of *Arhatship* very shortly. At that time the Bodhisattva Radiant Brightness was in the world and I went in my old age, leaning on a stick, to have an interview with him. My teacher [Pure Moon]

[173] Another name for the Western Paradise of Amitābha (Amida) Buddha.

scolded me, saying, "How mean, to esteem the son and slight the father!" At that time I did not think to have transgressed so asked the teacher to point it out. The teacher said, "As you were paying homage to the Bodhisattva Great Radiant Brightness your stick was leaning against a wall painting of the Buddha's face. Due to this negligence the second fruit of *Arhatship* was lost." I have punished my body with penances ever since and when I hear any evil speech it is like the wind, like shadows. Moreover, having been able to drink of the peerless sweet dew, why would one then perversely give rise to irritation? My only wish is, out of your great compassion, to pass on instruction in this wonderful Dharma.'

'You have cultivated many virtues for a long time,' said the Master, 'and you will continue my teaching. Listen to my *gatha*:'

To be in union with the Unborn through one word
Is to be united with the nature of the Dharma-realm.
If one can be liberated like this
Penetration of Relative and Absolute is complete.

Having transmitted the Dharma, Master Jāyatā did not arise from his seat but immediately returned to quiescence. Vasubandhu collected the *śarīra* relics and built a *stupa*. This was in the time of the Later Han dynasty, during the seventeenth year of the reign of Emperor Ming, corresponding to the eleventh year of the sexagenarian cycle.

2.28   Vasubandhu, the Twenty-First Patriarch

The twenty-first patriarch, Vasubandhu, was from Rajagrha and his family were of the merchant cast. His father's name was Covered in Light, his mother's The Dignified One. The family was prosperous but were without issue so both father and mother went to a Buddhist *stupa* to pray for an heir.

One night the mother dreamt that she swallowed two gems, one light, the other dark. When she awoke she was pregnant. After seven days an *Arhat* appeared by the name of Collected in Wisdom, who came to the house where the father, Covered in Light, welcomed him with courtesy. Arhat Collected in Wisdom, sitting formally, received the father's respects but when The Dignified One came out to pay her respects Collected in Wisdom rose from his cushion and said, 'Respects in turn to the Master of the Dharmakāya!' Father Covered in Light did not understand the cause, so taking a precious jewel, he knelt down and offered it to Arhat Collected in Wisdom, to test whether he was a true or a false *Arhat*. Collected in Wisdom received it without any gratitude at all. Covered in Light, unable to bear the situation asked, 'I am a gentleman, yet whilst extending respect to you, you ignore it. What then is the virtue of my wife that the Master ignores me?'

Arhat Collected in Wisdom answered, 'I accepted your respect and took the gem only to pass on good fortune to you, but your wife is carrying a boy who will be a sun of wisdom and a lamp in the world after he is born. That is why I ignored you. It was not giving preference to your wife.' The *Arhat* continued, 'Your wife will give birth to two sons, one to be called Vasubandhu – it was he whom I honoured. The second will be named Magpie. In ancient times the Tathāgata was practicing the Way in the Snowy Mountains (Himalayas) – a magpie had built its nest on one of its peaks. When the Buddha attained to the Way the magpie received its recompense by becoming the sovereign of the kingdom of Nadi. The Buddha predicted of him, "In the second five hundred year period [after my death] you will be born into a merchant family in Rajagrha and share the womb with a sage." Now it has come true.' After one month the two sons were born.

When the Master Vasubandhu reached his fifteenth year he prostrated before the Arhat Bright Liberation, left the home life and felt that it was Bodhisattva Vibhaha[174] (Pi Pohe) who conferred him with the full precepts.

On a missionary tour [Vasubandhu] journeyed to the kingdom of Nadi, where the king was called Ever Free. The king had two sons, the first one called Mahala, the second Manula. The king asked the Master, 'What is the difference in local customs between Rajagrha and here?'

The Master replied, 'Three Buddhas have come into the world in that country whilst in Your Majesty's kingdom now there are two spiritual leaders.'

'Who are these teachers?' asked the King.

The Master answered, 'The Buddha predicted that in the second five-hundred year period [after his death] a great spiritual man would appear in the world and leave the home life to follow the sage's calling. Manula, the second son of Your Majesty, is the first of these teachers; the other, although deficient in virtue, is myself.'

'If the case is honestly as you say,' said the King, 'then I now relinquish this son that he may become a monk.'

---

[174] 'The Limitless Bodhisattva'

'It is well! The great King is capable of following the intentions of the Buddha!' said the Master, who then gave Manula the full ordination and transmitted the Dharma to him with a *gatha*:

Bubbles and shadows are both without obstructions
So how could there not be awakening?
The penetration of dharmas goes through their middle
There is no present, there is no past.

Having finished the transmission Master Vasubandhu leapt with his body high up into the air and sat erect and firm as a mountain up there. The four assemblies looked up to him admiringly, and respectfully beseeched the Master to return to his cushion. Having seated himself down there in the crossed-legged position he passed away. They cremated him, collected the *śarīra* relics and erected a *stupa*.

This was in the twentieth year of the reign of Emperor Shang of the Later Han dynasty, corresponding to the fifty-fourth year of the sexagenarian cycle.

2.29 Manorhita, the Twenty-Second Patriarch

The twenty-second patriarch, Manorhita, was the son of the King Ever Free from the kingdom of Nadi. He first met the teacher Vasubandhu in his thirtieth year, when he left the home life and received the transmission.

He went to Western India to propagate the Dharma. In that country the king, called Gone Beyond, belonged to the Gautama clan. He took refuge in the Buddha vehicle and practiced seriously in it with great energy. One day whilst out walking he discovered a small *stupa* and wished to take it with him for a shrine but his entourage could not lift it. The King then called a great meeting of the three schools, the 'Noble Practitioners', the 'Dhyāna Meditators' and the 'Chanters' to clear up doubts. The Master also went to this meeting. None of the three groups was able to explain the phenomenon, so the Master, for the sake of the king, gave a detailed talk on the reasons for the *stupa* being thus. 'The appearance of the *stupa* just now is due to Your Majesty's prosperity and power,' said he.

The King, having heard these words said, 'To meet a supreme sage is difficult and worldly pleasures do not last for long.' Then he handed over the rule to the Crown Prince and, putting himself under the tutelage of the

Master, left the home life. After seven days he came to the fourth fruit of *Arhatship*.

The Master took great care over [the King's] instruction and said to him, 'You should stay in this country to properly liberate others. At present there is someone who is a great Dharma-vessel in a far off city whom I have to go and ordain.'

The King said, 'If the Master has to search him out in the ten directions could he not get there by moving his thoughts, rather than labour through the toil of going there in person?'

'It is indeed so,' said the Master. Thereupon he burnt incense and spoke to the monk Haklena (Kakurokuna) in distant Tukhāra saying, 'You, in that distant country, teaching and leading your congregation of cranes, the fruit of the Way should be experienced through your own understanding!' At that time Haklena was discoursing for the benefit of the king of that country, called King Treasure Seal, on some verses of a *sutra*. Suddenly, whilst gazing at the strange incense which was making shapes like clusters of fruit, the King said, 'What propitious sign is this?'

'This is nothing less than the Patriarch Manorhita from the western regions who is about to arrive with the transmission of the Buddha Heart Seal in its first perfumed descent to this country,' said Haklena.

'What kind of spiritual power does this Master [Manorhita] have?' asked the King.

'Concerning this Master,' said Haklena, 'a long time ago the Buddha predicted that it would be in this land that he would propagate widely the wonderful teaching.' Then the King [Treasure Seal] and Haklena both offered respectful greetings across the distance. Master [Manorhita, in Western India] was aware of this and then bade farewell to [the royal monk] Gone Beyond. He travelled in person to the kingdom of Tukhāra, where he received the homage from King Treasure Seal and Haklena.

Later Haklena asked the Master, 'Nine years had already passed living in the middle of a forest where I had a disciple called Dragon Son, who was young, clever and wise. I have looked into the depths of the three periods of time yet cannot learn of his origins.'

The Master said, 'Five *kalpas* ago this boy was born into a *Brahmin* family in the country Wonderful Joyful Kingdom. Once he made a donation of a piece of sandalwood for making a gong-striker to a Buddhist Temple and as a consequence became clever and respected by the assembly.'

Haklena also asked, 'And what affinity-links do I have that I feel for this assembly of cranes?'

'In the fourth *kalpa*',[175] the Master replied, 'you were a monk. You had to go to a meeting in the Dragon Palace and all your disciples wanted to go too, but you saw that not one of the five hundred was capable of taking part in the wonderful offering. The disciples then said, "The Master always said of the Dharma that those who share in eating share also in the Dharma. Now it is no more so. What wisdom does he have?" So you let them go to the meeting. Then you relinquished that life and took birth in other countries, transmitting the Dharma and your five hundred disciples, with their slight good fortune and feeble merit, were reborn as birds. That is why, in response to your former benevolence, they are an assembly of cranes which are following you.'

Haklena, on hearing this, said, 'With what skilful means may they be liberated then?'

'I have the peerless Treasure of the Dharma; you should listen and take it in, so as to use the coming opportunity,' said the Master, and then recited a *gatha*:

The heart flows with the cycles of the ten-thousand things,
These cycles are truly mysterious.
Follow the flow and know,
The True Nature is without joy or sorrow.

When the flock of cranes heard this *gatha* they took off and flew away. The Master sat cross-legged on his cushion and peacefully entered transformation. Haklena and King Treasure Seal set up a *stupa*. This was in the seventeenth year of Emperor Huan of the Later Han dynasty, corresponding to the forty-second year of the sexagenarian cycle.

2.30 Haklena (Kakurokuna), the Twenty-Third Patriarch

The twenty-third patriarch, Haklena, (Textual Comment: *Le-na* is a Sanskrit name, whilst *he* [crow] is a Chinese one; because the Master, when he came into the world, had formerly forged a feeling connection with a flock of cranes and their tender attach-

---

[175] The four *kalpas*, or epochs of a world are formation, stability, destruction and annihilation. (DCBT: 171a.)

ment persisted, his appellation is 'Crow' – *he*) was from the kingdom of Tukhāra. The family was of the *Brahmin* cast; his father's name was Thousand Victories and his mother's Golden Light. Being without children, she prayed before the golden banners of the Seven Buddhas. Then she dreamt of a spiritual child atop Mount Sumeru, supporting a golden halo, saying 'I am coming.' On waking up she found that she was pregnant.

When he was seven years old, Haklena was wandering about and came to a village where he saw people worshiping improperly, so he entered the temple to scold them. He said, 'You presumptuously raise expectations of calamity and good fortune by deluding and misleading people, sacrificing animals for years in vain. This is very harmful behaviour.' No sooner were his words spoken than the temple collapsed, so the villagers called him The Child Sage.

At twenty-two Haklena left the home life and at thirty he met Master Manorhita, who transmitted the treasury of the Dharma-eye to him.

On a missionary tour in Central India, the king there was called Fearless Ocean and he was greatly devoted to the Buddha's Way. Once, when the Master was discoursing on the True Dharma for him, the King suddenly saw two men, the one wearing crimson, the other, white robes, bowing to the Master. The King asked, 'Who are these men?'

'These are the divine sons, Sun and Moon,' said the Master, 'I discoursed once, a long time ago, on the Dharma to them, which is why they have come to pay their respects.' After a while they were no longer visible, only a strange perfume lingered.

'What is the extent of Sun and Moon's territory?' asked the King.

'In every universe where the One Thousand Buddhas preach,' said the Master, 'there are one hundred thousand suns and moons and Sumeru Mountains. If I were to give details of these, the description would never come to an end.'

The King heard this with delight.

At that time the Master discoursed on the Supreme Way, liberating the many who were ready for it. The [Master's] most senior disciple, Dragon, died young but he had an elder brother, called Lion, learned in many things and with a very good memory. He had served a *Brahmin* until he also died, thus leaving him with a double loss [of his younger brother and then his *Brahmin* teacher]. Then he went to take refuge with Master Haklena by asking him, 'I wish to seek the Way, so how should one employ the Heart?'

'If you wish to seek the Way.' said the Master, 'there is no Heart which should be employed.'

'Since there is no Heart to be employed,' countered Lion, 'who then does the Buddhist practice?'

'If you have to employ something,' the Master replied, 'that is not meritorious. If you have nothing to do, then that is the work of the Buddha. A *sutra* says, "The merit which I do is due to the absence of 'I'".'

After Lion had heard this he immediately gained access to the Wisdom of the Buddhas.

Once, the Master suddenly pointed in the direction of the northwest saying, 'What is that in the sky?'

Lion said, 'I see in the sky something like a white rainbow arching through heaven and earth and there is also black sky with five horizontal lines going across its middle.'

'What does this omen mean?' asked the Master.

'It really cannot be fathomed,' said Lion.

The Master said, 'Fifty years after my death in a northern kingdom of India there will arise some difficulties which will be detrimental to yourself. I shall die soon, so now the Dharma-eye is entrusted to you. Take good care of yourself.' Then he recited a *gatha*:

When the nature of the heart is realised
One could say that it is inconceivable.
Clearly understood, there is nothing to be attained
On attaining it one does not talk of knowing.

When the monk, Lion, heard this *gatha* he was happy and content, but he still did not know what difficulty was to befall him. The Master then revealed it to him privately. Having finished with the discourse [the Master] manifested the eighteen transformations and then returned to quiescence. After the cremation[176] the *śarīra* relics were divided and each party wished to set up a *stupa*. The Master then appeared once more in the air and recited this *gatha*:

One Dharma is all dharmas
All dharmas are units of a single Dharma.
My body is neither existent nor non-existent
Why divide it into so many *stupas*?

[176] *Jhāpita*, a monk's cremation, DCBT.463b.C

124

When the great assembly heard this *gatha* they discontinued dividing the relics and set up the *stupa* in the capital.

This was in the twenty-first year of the reign of Emperor Xian of the Later Han, corresponding to the twenty-sixth year of the sexagenarian cycle.

2.31 Āryasimha (Lion of the Āryas), the Twenty-Fourth Patriarch [177]

The twenty-fourth patriarch, Āryasimha, was a man from Central India whose family belonged to the *Brahmin* cast. Having received the transmission he came to Kashmir on his missionary tour. There someone called Harika originally practiced Dhyāna introspection, as a result of which five sects arose – those who practiced meditation, those who sought after knowledge, those who held to form, those who rejected form and those who kept silence.

The Master asked about this, as a result of which four of the group silently and willingly followed the line of Āryasimha. Only Dharmadatta, the leader of the meditation group, on hearing of the four sects being taken to task, became angry, so he came [to see the Master].

The Master said, 'The Venerable Sir is practicing meditation, so why should he come here? Since he has come what does that say about "practicing meditation"?'

'Although I have come here my heart is not confused,' replied Dharmadatta. 'Meditation goes according to the man who is training in it. What does it have to do with place?'

The Master said, 'Since the Venerable Sir has come, his training has also arrived. If there were no such thing, where is the man's training?'

'Meditation trains the man, it is not the man who trains meditation,' said Dharmadatta. 'Although I come here, this meditation is always training [the man].'

The master said, 'So the man is not training in meditation but the meditation trains the man. When the man himself comes here, then who trains in this meditation?'

Dharmadatta said, 'It is like a pure bright pearl in which there is no opaque-

---

[177] For a discussion on an influential earlier transmission text which terminates with the murder of Simha Bhikṣu (T.2058, 'Account of the Transmission of the Dharma Treasury') see Wendy Adamek, MT:101-110 and **(3.40)**, the biography of Sengcan, the 3rd Chinese Patriarch of Chan.

ness inside or outside. Meditation, if penetrated and understood, should be like this.'

'If meditation is penetrated and understood,' said the Master, 'it resembles a bright gem indeed, but on observing the Venerable Sir's, it is not the gem of a disciple.'

Dharmadatta said, 'The brightness of this gem penetrates inside and outside, so all is meditation. My heart is not confused. It is just like this purity.'

'Since this gem has no inside or outside,' said the Master, 'how is the Venerable Sir capable of meditation? Although the defilements are without movement or wavering, this meditation is not that [immovable] purity.'

Dharmadatta, thus confronted by the Master, was enlightened and his heart became clear and bright.

Having united the five schools the Master's reputation spread far and wide.

Whilst searching for a Dharma-heir [Master Āryasimha] came across an old man who brought his son with him. The man said to the Master, 'This son is called Śita (Siduo) and when he was born his left hand was a clenched fist, yet even now, since growing up, he's never been able to open it. Would that the Master might reveal the *karmic* cause of this.'

The Master looked at the boy and taking his hand said, 'You can return my jewel now!' The boy suddenly opened his hand and presented him with a jewel. The whole assembly was astonished. The Master said, 'In a former life I was a monk and had a young attendant by the name of Vaśya (Bashya, Poshe). Once I went to the Western Sea to attend a feast and was given a valuable pearl, which I entrusted to him. Now he is returning the pearl. This is as it should be.' The old man then let his son leave the home life, whereupon the Master gave him the precepts and in accordance with their affinity links, named him Vaśyaśita (Bashyashita). The Master then said to him, 'My teacher privately predicted, rather anxiously, that a calamity would befall me before long, so I now transmit to you the Treasury of the True Dharma-eye of the Tathāgata. You should guard it well so that it may flourish everywhere in the coming time. This is the *gatha*:'

When speaking truly about knowing-awareness
The knowing-awareness is all Heart.
Since it is heart that is knowing-awareness
Knowing-awareness is the present moment.

When the Master had finished reciting the *gatha*, he privately handed over his robe to Bashyashita, enjoining him to propagate the teaching in countries according to their need. On receiving these instructions he left directly for Southern India.

Since the Master could no longer avoid the disaster coming to him, he remained alone in Kashmir. Now in that country at the time there were two heretics, one called Mamokuta, the other Torakusha. They had studied all the arts of magic and wished to plot revolution together. Disguised then as Buddhist monks, they stealthily entered the King's palace, reasoning thus, 'If we don't succeed then the crime will be put down to the Buddhists.' But evildoers are their own undoing and calamity rebounded on them – they were caught for their deeds. But the King was angry and said, 'We have always taken refuge in the Three Jewels, so how could such harm as this visit us?' Then he ordered the destruction of Buddhist Temples, expelled all the assemblies and, himself brandishing a sword, went to the place where the Master [Āryasimha] was staying and asked him, 'Has the Teacher attained to the emptiness of the *five skandhas* or not?'

'The emptiness of the *five skandhas* has already been attained,' replied the Master.

'And indifference to life and death?' asked the King.

'Indifference to life and death too,' replied the Master.

'Since you are indifferent to life and death,' said the King, 'can you give me your head?'

'This body is not my possession,' replied the Master, 'so why be stingy with its head?'

The King then, wielding his sword, cut off the Master's head. White milk spurted out of his body to a height of several feet. The King's right arm immediately twisted round and fell to the ground. Seven days later he was dead.

The Crown Prince Head of Radiance sighed and said, 'Why did my father take such calamity upon himself?' At that time there was a hermit living in the White Elephant Mountains with a profound understanding of the law of cause and effect. To free the Prince from doubts, he explained to him in detail the causes stemming from a previous life. A *stupa* was built as retribution for the body of Master Āryasimha.

This was in the twentieth year of the reign of Emperor Qi of the Wei dynasty, corresponding to the sixteenth year of the sexagenarian cycle.

Besides making Bashyashita his legitimate heir by transmitting the Dharma of the Heart and the Robe of Faith, Master Āryasimha also produced, through Dharmadatta, twenty-two masters over four generations.

2.32 Bashyashita, the Twenty-fifth Patriarch

The twenty-fifth patriarch, Bashyashita, was a native of Kashmir whose family belonged to the *Brahmin* cast. His father's name was Tranquil Walker, his mother's Ever Content. She became pregnant after having a dream of obtaining a divine sword. When he was born his left hand was clenched in a fist. On meeting Master Āryasimha the cause of this was revealed as being from a previous life.

Having received the Heart Seal Transmission in secret, he first travelled to Southern India and then to Central India. The name of the king in this country was Kāśyapā, who courteously provided him support. At that time there was a heretic called Selflessly Holy who, because of the King's courteous attentions, was jealous of the arrival of the patriarch. He wished to have a debate with him so as to be in the royal favour by winning it, thus consolidating his case. Then in the King's presence he said to the Patriarch, 'I understand the silent debate which does not rely on words.'

The Patriarch replied, 'Who knows the winner and the loser?'

'It is not about winning and losing,' said the heretic, 'it is only about meaning.'

'What do you take as the meaning?' asked the Patriarch.

'No-Heart is the meaning,' said the heretic.

'How can one obtain a meaning from No-Heart?' asked the Patriarch.

'When I talk of "No-Heart" it is taken as a name, not a meaning,' replied the heretic.

'You talk of "No-Heart", taking it only as a name, not as a meaning,' said the Patriarch. 'I say, "It is not a Heart" and take that as the meaning, not a name.'

'If the meaning is taken as not being a name then who could discern the meaning?' asked the heretic.

Your name has no meaning,' replied the Patriarch, 'so what kind of name is this name?'

'By discerning no meaning, this name is no name,' replied the heretic.

'If the name is not a name and meaning is equally not a meaning, then who discerns what?' asked the Patriarch. In this way the debate went backwards and forwards for fifty-nine times until the heretic shut his mouth and yielded in good faith.

Once the Patriarch suddenly turned to the north and, palms together, he sighed, saying, 'My teacher, Master Āryasimha, has today met with his calamity. This is such a disaster for him!' Then taking his leave of the King, he went south until he reached Southern India and the valleys of the Silent Mountains. In this country the king of that time was called Heavenly Virtue. He welcomed the Patriarch and offered him sustenance. The King had two sons; the first was bad and violent but his physical strength was abundant. The other son was amiable but sickly from infancy on. The Patriarch gave an explanation of the causes for this, so that the King's doubts were immediately dispelled.

There was also a teacher at court who was an expert in exorcising ghosts and who was jealous of the Patriarch's way. He secretly placed poisoned herbs in his food and drink. The Patriarch knew of this but ate it nonetheless and this backfired to the teacher, who got the misfortune. But then, by submitting to the Patriarch, he left the home life and received the full precepts.

Sixty[?] years later the Crown Prince succeeded to the throne as Virtuous Conqueror. Again the heretics were popular at court, causing difficulties for the Patriarch. The present Crown Prince, Punyamitra, having approached the throne to admonish the King, was imprisoned. Then the King suddenly asked the Patriarch, 'Until now my country has had nothing to do with superstitious aberrations. What doctrines does the teacher pass on?'

The Patriarch answered, 'Indeed Your Majesty's country has from of old had really nothing to do with evil dharmas. What I have come to is the teaching of the Buddha.'

'The Buddha has already been dead for one thousand two hundred years,' said the King, 'so from whom has the teacher obtained this teaching?'

'Great Master Drinking Light (Mahākāśyapā) personally received the seal of the Buddha,' said the Patriarch, 'and from him it was passed on for twenty-four generations until it reached Master Āryasimha. I obtained the transmission from him.'

'We have heard that this teacher could not avoid being decapitated,' said the King, 'so how can he have transmitted the Dharma on to the next person?'

'My Master's difficulties had not yet arisen at the time when he secretly transmitted the Robe of Faith and the *gatha*, with which I can prove the inheritance of my teacher,' said the Patriarch.

'Where is the Robe?' asked the King. The Patriarch then took the Robe from its bag and showed it to the King. The King ordered it to be burnt, but the five colours of the rainbow were brilliant; when the fire had exhausted itself [the Robe] was as before. The King was then full of remorse and apologised profusely. Now that it was clear that the teacher was the true heir [of Master Āryasimha], he released the Crown Prince.

The Crown Prince then sought to become a monk so the Patriarch questioned him, 'You wish to renounce the home life. For what reason?'

'If I were to renounce the home life it would not be for something special,' replied the Prince.

'What things would you refrain from?' asked the Patriarch.

'To refrain from doing worldly things,' replied the Prince.

'And what things would you do?' asked the Patriarch

'I would see to the affairs of the Buddha,' answered the Crown Prince.

'The Crown Prince's sagacity is very great. He must be in the line of all the sages!' said the Patriarch. Then he was allowed to leave the home life and was for six years [the Master's] attendant, after which he received the full precepts in the Royal Palace. On the occasion of the ordination the great earth trembled and there were quite a few other miraculous signs.

The Patriarch told Punyamitra, 'I am already feeble and decrepit. How is it possible to remain any longer? You must guard well the Treasury of the True Dharma-eye and liberate all sentient beings. Listen to my *gatha*:'

The sage talks of knowing-awareness
In the world it is neither right nor wrong.
As I realise the True Nature now
It is neither a path nor a principle.

Punyamitra listened and then said to the Patriarch, 'It is fitting to transmit the Robe.'

The Patriarch replied, 'This Robe was for the sake of a temporary testimony to the calamity. But your person is without calamity so why use the Robe? Propagate in all the ten directions and people will follow out of faith.' After hearing these words Punyamitra bowed and withdrew.

The Patriarch manifested the spiritual transformations and transformed by the Samadhi fire, cremated himself. The *śarīra* relics came to be one foot in height and King Virtuous Conqueror built a *stupa* in which to secrete them.

This was in the reign of Emperor Ming of the Eastern Qin dynasty in the third year of the Tai'ning era, corresponding to the twenty-second year of the sexagenarian cycle.

2.33 Punyamitra, the Twenty-Sixth Patriarch

The twenty-sixth patriarch, Punyamitra, was the heir to the throne of King Virtuous Conqueror of Southern India. On being ordained and receiving the Dharma he went to East India. The King there, called Firm and Sure, had a long-nailed heretic *Brahmin* as teacher. When the Master was approaching [the region] the King and his ascetic *Brahmin* both saw a luminous white light piercing heaven and earth. The King said, 'What is this auspicious sign?' The ascetic already knew that it was the Master entering the region and fearing that the King might change to someone better he said, 'It is actually the sign of a demon coming. How could it be auspicious?' Then he summoned all his followers to a meeting saying, 'Punyamitra is about to enter the city. Who can block him?' A disciple said, 'We have each our arts of sorcery with which we can move heaven and earth, enter fire and water, so what is there to fear?'

As the Master arrived he first saw a black cloud around the palace walls and said, 'There's a little trouble here!' and then proceeded directly to the King's palace.

'For what reason has the Master come here?' asked the King.

'In order to liberate sentient beings,' replied the Master.

'To liberate by which Dharma?' asked the King.

'I liberate each according to their need,' replied the Master.

The ascetic *Brahmin*, having heard this dialogue, could not contain his anger and so, with his magic powers, he transformed himself into a great mountain sitting on top of the Master's head. But when the Master pointed to it, it suddenly moved over the heads of the ascetic's own gathering. He and his group were afraid and submitted to the Master. The Master took pity on their foolishness and pointed again at the magic mountain, which immediately collapsed and disappeared.

Then he expounded on the essentials of the Dharma to the King, enabling him to hasten towards the True Vehicle. He also said to the King, 'There is a sage in this country and he will succeed me!'

At that time there lived in that country the son of a *Brahmin*, about twenty years old, who had already lost his mother and father when he was young. He didn't know his family name but called himself Precious Necklace, so people called him Precious Necklace Boy. He wandered about the neighbourhood begging for alms to keep alive, in the manner of those who never cause offence to others. When someone asked him, 'Why do you walk so quickly?' he would reply, 'Why do you walk so slowly?' or when asked about his name he would say, 'The same name as you.' Nobody knew why.

One day the King was out in the carriage with the Master. They saw Precious Necklace Boy bowing in front of them. The Master said to him, 'Do you remember things of the past or not?'

'I remember in a *kalpa* long ago living with the Master in the same abode,' said Precious Necklace Boy, 'the Master was discoursing on the Great Wisdom whilst I was turning the extremely profound *sutra*. Today's events are in accord with those ancient causes.'

The Master said to the King, 'This boy is none other than the Bodhisattva Mahāstāmaprāpta[178] and through this sage two men will go into the world to propagate the Dharma, one in Southern India, whilst the other will have a *karmic* affinity with China; but after four or five years he will want to return to this region.' Thus, because of his old affinity with the Master, the boy was given the name Prajñātara (Skt. Hannyatara) and the Master transmitted the treasury of the Dharma-eye to him with a *gatha*:

The True Nature is the treasury of the Heart -ground
It has neither head nor tail.
Affinity is a condition for the transformation of things
For convenience it is called wisdom.

Having transmitted the Dharma the Master took leave of the King saying, 'My affinity-transmission is completed. Now it is time to return to the realm of cessation. May Your Majesty not forget to protect the Supreme Vehicle.' Then he returned to his seat and, sitting in the lotus posture, passed away. Transforming into fire, he cremated himself. The King collected the *śarīra* relics and had a *stupa* in which to bury them.

This was in the reign of the Emperor Xiao Wu of the Eastern Qin dynasty in the sixteenth year of the Taiyuan era, corresponding to the twenty-fifth year of the sexagenarian cycle.

---

[178] A powerful Bodhisattva, Mahāstāmaprāpta is symbolised by the moon (wisdom) while Avalokiteśvara is symbolised by the sun (compassion).

2.34 Prajñātara, the Twenty-Seventh Patriarch

The twenty-seventh patriarch, Prajñātara, was a native of Eastern India. After receiving the Dharma he went on a missionary tour to Southern India. The king's name there was Excelling in Fragrance and he venerated the Buddha vehicle, reverenced and supported it beyond the normal, even to the bestowal of a priceless jewel on the Master.

At the time the King had three sons, the youngest of whom was an enlightened one. The Master wished to test their attainments so taking the jewel, he asked the three sons of the King, 'This jewel is bright and perfect, is there something which can measure up to it or not?' The first son, Prince Pure-Eyed Tara, and the second son, Prince Meritorious Virtue Tara, both said, 'This is the most valuable of the seven jewels and there is certainly nothing that could surpass it. Who except the Master's spiritual strength would be able to receive it?'

The third son Bodhitara said, 'This is a mundane treasure. It falls short of the supreme one. Of all treasures, the treasure of the Dharma is supreme. This has a mundane lustre, and falls short of the supreme. Of all these, the lustre of Wisdom is supreme. This has a mundane bright penetration but falls short of the supreme one. Of all penetrations the bright penetration of the Heart is supreme. This jewel's brightness cannot shine forth of itself; it needs the support of the light of Wisdom so that the light can distinguish things. To be able to distinguish like this is to know that it is a jewel, to know that it is a jewel is to distinguish it as a treasure. Being able to distinguish its treasure, it is treasured as a treasure that is not of self. Able to distinguish this jewel, the jewel is not a jewel of the worldly self. The jewel that is not a jewel of the self needs the support of the jewel of Wisdom to distinguish it from the worldly jewel. The treasure that is not a treasure of the self needs the support of the Treasure of Wisdom with which to clarify the Treasure of the Dharma. This being so, the Master himself has become this Way, so its treasure can manifest. When living beings become the Way, the treasure of their Hearts will manifest like this too!'

The Master sighed in wonder at the penetration of Bodhitara's wisdom and questioning him further asked, 'What, of all things, is the thing without characteristic marks?'

'Amongst all things, non-arising is without any characteristic marks,' replied Bodhitara.

Again the Master asked, 'Amongst all things, which thing is the most high?'

'Amongst all things, the human being is the most high,' replied Bodhitara.

Again the Master questioned him, 'Amongst all things which is the very greatest?'

'The very greatest amongst all things is the Dharma-nature,' replied Bodhitara.

The Master knew then that this was his Dharma-heir, but that the time had not yet arrived so he kept silent and had Bodhitara mingle amongst them.

Then King Excelling in Fragrance died and all his entourage mourned him. Only the third son, Bodhitara, entered into meditation in front of the King's coffin and after the passage of seven days came out of it. Then he wished to leave the home life so received the full precepts from the Master, who said to him, 'The Tathāgata transmitted the True Dharma-eye to Mahākāśyapā, and thus it has been passed down until it came to me. I now entrust it to you, so listen to my *gatha*:'

In Heart-ground arise all seeds;
Due to phenomena principle also arises.
Fruit ripened is *Bodhi* completed –
The flower opens and worlds arise.

Having transmitted the Dharma the Master rose from his seat and stretching out his hands to each side, twenty-seven bright rays of dazzling multi-coloured light streamed out from each hand. Then he sprang himself into the air, to the height of seven palm trees, and transformed into fire. From heaven the *śarīra* relics came down like rain and collected, a *stupa* was built for them.

This was in the first year of the era of Great Clarity, in the reign of the Emperor Xiao Wu of the Song dynasty, corresponding to the thirty-fourth year of the sexagenarian cycle (457 CE).

End of Book Two

Book Three

3.35 Bodhidharma, the Twenty-Eighth Patriarch, the First Chinese Patriarch of Chan

The twenty-eighth patriarch, Bodhidharma, was the third son of Excelling in Fragrance, the King of a country in Southern India. His family was of the noble cast and originally his name was Bodhitara. Later he met the twenty-seventh patriarch Prajñātara, who had arrived in his country and had been offered royal patronage. Knowing of [Bodhitara's] hidden path, Prajñātara had him tested, together with his two brothers, about his discernment regarding the jewel bestowed upon him [by the king] and the clarity of his spiritual essence. Having done that Master Prajñātara then said to [Bodhitara], 'You have already penetrated all the teachings, so "Dharma" has penetrated to the great understanding. Fitting is it then to be called Dharma.' His name was then changed to Bodhidharma.

The teacher, Bodhidharma, then asked Master Prajñātara, 'Now that I have attained to the Dharma, which country is it necessary to go to in order to promote the Buddha's practice? Please be so kind as to give an indication.'

The Master said, 'Although you have attained to the Dharma you cannot yet travel far, so remain in Southern India. Wait until after my death at the age of sixty-seven, and then go to China. By establishing the medicine of the Great Dharma there, you will make direct contact with men of superior roots. Be prudent and do not be in a hurry to go there, for the capital is in decline.'

Bodhidharma said, 'Are there, in that country, great beings who would be deep vessels of the Dharma or not? And will there be any calamities in the next thousand years?'

The Master answered, 'In the countries where your missionary activities will take place, those who will obtain *Bodhi* will be countless. About sixty years after my death there will be difficulties in that country to do with waves of water and you yourself would do well to submit to these. When you reach China do not stay in the south for they only consider success to be good and have no regard for the principles of Buddhism. Even if the south is to be your place of arrival, you cannot stay there very long. Listen to my *gatha*:'

On the road, crossing the waters, you will meet a sheep,[179]
Alone and aggrieved, in darkness you will cross a river.

---

[179] A possible reference to Yangcheng (lit. sheep city), another name for Guangzhou, a city in the south of China.

At the capital you take pity on an elephant and a horse, [180]
Two young cassia trees will prosper for a long time.

Then he recited eight further *gathas*, all of which prophesied the future rise and fall of the Buddha's teaching (all these matters are discussed in the 'Transmissions from the Precious Forest'[181] and in 'Collection of the Heirs of the Sage').

Respectfully imbibing the import of the teachings, Bodhidharma worked diligently as attendant to the Master for almost forty years, never neglecting his duties, right up to Master Prajñātara's death, after which he made the training available in his native land.

At that time there were two other teachers [in India], the one whose name was Buddha Greatly Advanced, the other whose name was Great Excellent Buddha and together they had trained under their teacher Buddhabhadra[182] in the meditation techniques of the Small Vehicle. After Buddha Greatly Advanced had come across Prajñātara, he speedily forsook the Small Vehicle for the greater one. Later, teacher and pupil were famous everywhere as the two entrances to the sweet dew of the Dharma, whilst the teaching of Great Excellent Buddha split into six different sects. The first of these six sects was the Sect of Form; the second, the Formless Sect; the third, the Sect of Samādhi and Wisdom; the fourth, the Vinaya-Discipline Sect; the fifth, the Nothing-to-Attain Sect; the sixth, the Quiescent and Tranquil Sect. Each of these sects was locked into its own interpretations, teaching differently the single source and falling into making lofty distinctions; their followers were many.

The great teacher (Bodhidharma) sighed deeply and lamented, 'Their teacher fell into the ox's shit, how they prosper in confusion, even splitting up into six sects! If I do not do away with this situation they will be forever entangled in wrong views!' Having spoken thus, he appeared before the assembly of

---

[180] A possible reference to an ancient mausoleum or burial mound guarded by two stone animals, an elephant and a horse, facing each other, at the site of a desolated capital after being sacked, pillaged and ravaged by war. – See note 201 below.

[181] Parts of this work, namely chapters 1-6 and 8, were discovered in 1932. Chapters 7, 9 and 10 have yet to be found. PSS: 47, n.165.

[182] Interestingly, in China at the same time there were two named Buddhabhadra in the 5th century; one was the first abbot of the Shaolin Temple, the other, the translator (359-429 CE) of the *Avatamsaka Sutra*. It is not known if there were others: in any case, there is an interesting confusion between a Buddhabhadra (whose biography is in T. 50, [2060] 551a21-b26) and Bodhidharma; see MT: 141.

the first Sect of Form in his rather formidable presence and asked them, 'Of all phenomena which can be called the True Form?'

Amongst this assembly was an elder named Sabara who answered, 'Amongst all forms the one which has no reciprocal action with any other form is called the True Form.'

The master (Bodhidharma) said, 'If what is called the True Form is the one which, amongst all forms, has no reciprocal action with any other, then how is that ascertained?'

The other replied, 'Amongst all forms the true one is neither permanent nor impermanent. If there were something permanent in any phenomenon, how could that be called true?'

The master said, 'So all forms which are impermanent are called True Forms? Since you are at this moment impermanent, how did you obtain this [True Form]?'

The other replied, 'I am talking about impermanence, not discussing all forms, but if we are talking about all forms, the meaning is the same.'

The master said, 'You talk of impermanence as being the True Form, but there is no true form in either permanence or impermanence.'

The other replied, 'Since this permanence is also impermanent, it is therefore not the True Form. Like knowing that I *is not*, being neither permanent nor impermanent.'

The master said, 'If at this moment you do not change is this then called the True Form? But you have changed already, have moved on already – this is the meaning too!'

The other replied, '"Unchanging" only exists because it both exists and does not exist, therefore change is the True Form and it takes permanence as its principle.'

The master said, 'If True Form does not change, it means change is not the true, so amongst things both existent and non-existent, what is called the True Form?'

Sabara's heart realised the wisdom of the master's deep and penetrating insight. Pointing his hand into the empty sky he said, 'This is a form existing in the world, yet it can also be empty, cannot my body be like this too?'

The master said, 'If one has penetrated True Form then it is seen to be no-Form. If one penetrates no-Form, its form is also like this. In the midst of form, the essence of Form is not lost; in the midst of no-Form, nothing obstructs its being. If one can understand this, this is called True Form.'

In hearing this, the hearts of the whole assembly were clarified and, bowing respectfully, they faithfully adopted the teachings.

The master then, his traces disappearing in a flash, came to the place of the second, the Formless Sect. He asked them, 'You speak about Formlessness, what do you take as proof of it?'

In that assembly there was a wise one called Paradhi, who answered, 'I understand Formlessness as the non-arising of the Heart.'

The master said, 'If your Heart does not arise then how do you understand that?'

The other answered, 'I understand Formlessness as the Heart which neither grasps at nor rejects anything. At the same time this understanding is not a thing.'

The master said, 'If the heart, in all things existent or non-existent, neither grasps at nor rejects anything, and if there is also no one who understands, then there is absolutely no understanding either.'

The other replied, 'Even entering Buddha's three samādhis, there is no place to get to, how much the more so Formlessness and the desire to know it.'

The master said, 'Since form is not known, who is it that is talking about existence and non-existence? Further, if there is no place to get to, how can that be called the three samādhis?'

The other replied, 'My talking does not prove it, for the proof is without proof. There are no three samādhis, though I talk of three samādhis.'

The master said, 'There being no three samādhis, who is giving a name to them? Since you do not prove anything, why prove that there is no proof?'

Paradhi, on hearing the master's penetrating analysis, awakened to his original Heart and bowing respectfully to the master, entreated him to forgive his erroneous ways.

The master predicted, 'You will soon obtain the fruit and prove it for yourself and before long subdue an evil spirit in this country.' Having spoken he suddenly disappeared.

Arriving at the place of the third, Samādhi and Wisdom Sect, the master asked them, 'You practice Samādhi and Wisdom; are they one or are they two?'

Amongst the assembly there was one called Barandha, who answered, 'Our Samādhi and Wisdom is neither one nor two.'

The master said, 'Since it is neither one nor two, why call it Samādhi-Wisdom?'

The other replied, 'It is in samādhi, yet it is not samādhi, it is being wise, yet it is not wise. Since one is not one, two is also not two.'

The master said, 'Taking one as not being one and two as not being two, and there being no Samādhi-Wisdom, what then, simply, is Samādhi-Wisdom?'

The other answered, 'It is not one, it is not two – Samādhi-Wisdom can know this; being neither samādhi nor wisdom is also like this.'

The master said, 'Because wisdom is not samādhi, how can it be known that they are neither one nor two, or which is samādhi and which is wisdom?'

Barandha's doubting heart, on hearing this, melted away like ice. Coming to the fourth, the Vinaya-Discipline Sect, the master asked, 'What is called Vinaya, what is called Discipline? Do you take this Vinaya-Discipline to be one or two?'

Amongst the assembly was a wise man, who answered, 'One, two, or two and one, these are all things which are subject to arising. To rely on the teaching and be without defilements, this is called Vinaya-Discipline.'

The master said, 'You talk of relying on the teaching, but just this is the defilement, for unless "one" and "two" are both broken through, how can one talk of relying on the teaching? This dualistic disobedience is not Discipline, and inside and outside not being clear, how can that be called the Vinaya?'

The other said, 'I exist inside and outside – this is already known; to have penetrated this is already the Vinaya-Discipline. If you talk of disobedience, then that is both right and wrong but if speech is pure, it conforms to both Vinaya and Discipline.'

The master said, 'If everything is both right and wrong then how can speech be pure? If this has already been understood, how is it possible to babble about outside and inside?'

The wise one, on hearing this, felt embarrassed and submitted.

Coming to the place of the fifth, Nothing-to-Attain Sect, the master asked them, 'You say "there is nothing to attain" – what is the attainment of "there is nothing to attain?" Since there is nothing that can be attained there is also no attainment of [the state of] "there is nothing to attain" '.

Amongst the assembly was one called Priceless Purity, who answered, 'I say that there is nothing to attain, but "nothing to attain" is not an attainment. When talking of attaining this attainment, it is the attainment of there being nothing to attain.'

The master answered, 'Since the attainment is not to attain, attainment is also non-attainment. Yet when you talk of attaining this attainment, what kind of attaining of this attainment is attained?'

The other replied, 'Understand that attainment is non-attainment, then non-attainment is the attainment. If it is understood as not attained, this is called attaining that attainment.'

The master said, 'Since what is attained is a non-attainment, attained is the attainment of there being nothing to attain. Since there is nothing that can be attained, then what attainment is attained to?'

On hearing this, Priceless Purity's net of doubts was suddenly destroyed.

Coming to the place of the sixth, Quiescent and Tranquil Sect, the master asked them, 'What do you call Quiescent and Tranquil? In this Dharma, what is Tranquil, what is Quiescent?'

There was a venerable one there who answered, 'If this heart does not move, this is called Quiescent; if there are no defilements in the dharmas , this is called Tranquillity.'

The master said, 'If the Original Heart were not by nature quiescent, it would have to be a sham Quiescence, but because originally it is quiescent by nature, then what is the use of your "Quiescence"?'

The other answered, 'All dharmas are originally empty and because emptiness is empty, that emptiness of the empty is referred to as Tranquillity.'

The master said, 'The emptiness of empty is completely empty. All the dharmas are also like this, tranquil and without form, so what could be "Quiescent", what "Tranquil"?'

Having heard the master pointing out this teaching, the Venerable One was suddenly enlightened.

Then the six sects swore an oath to take refuge in the teachings and due to this the master's influence covered southern India and his reputation spread across the whole country so that students from far and near inclined towards his teachings. For more than sixty years an innumerable number of beings were led across to the other shore.

Later it happened that the king, who had heretical views, became destructive towards the three treasures, often saying, 'Our ancestors all had faith in the Buddha's Way, but falling into such erroneous ways their life-spans were not longer and their blessings were erratic. Moreover, if I myself am Buddha, why then search any further? Recompense for good and evil arises due to sly talk of those who are too clever.'

As to the elders in the country who had formerly been esteemed by the king, they were all dismissed.

The master, knowing of the situation, sighed deeply on account of the barrenness of the king's virtue and wondered how he could save him. Then he thought again about the two leaders of the Formless Sect, the first of whom, Paradhi, had a strong relationship with the king, which was about to come to fruition. The second leader, Spiritual Excellence, although not without eloquence, had had no previous connection [with the king]. Also, each of the followers of the six sects thought 'the Buddha-dharma is in difficulties – why does the Master not arrange something.'

While the master was far away, he still knew of the assemblies' intentions and responded by snapping his fingers. The six assemblies heard this and said, 'This is the signal from our Master Bodhidharma to us. It is necessary that we go immediately in aid to his kind summons.'

Having said this, they arrived at the master's place and bowing reverently before him made enquiries. The master said, 'At present there is a leaf in the hazy sky. Who would be capable of expelling it?'

Spiritual Excellence said, 'Although shallow in understanding, dare I shrink from taking action?'

The master said, 'While you are wise in analysis, the spiritual power is still not ripe yet.'

Spiritual Excellence thought to himself, 'The master fears that I will see the king and perform the great Buddhist work [of converting him], thereby winning renown for my name and snatching away his venerable authority. Even if he is crowned with good fortune and wisdom, I am a monk who has received the message of the Buddhist teachings, so would it be so difficult to oppose him?' Having thus taken counsel with himself he secretly left and arrived before the king. Extensively he preached to him the essentials of the Dharma, of the miseries and enjoyments of the world, and of such things as the good and bad in man and in heavenly beings. Although the king asked questions at every turn, Spiritual Excellence did not lose sight of the principle.

The king asked, 'Where is the Dharma that you have just now made understandable?'

Spiritual Excellence replied, 'It is like the transformative power of Your Majesty's rule, it should be in accord with its Dao. Where is the Dao which belongs to Your Majesty?'

The king said, 'The Dao to which I belong consists of rooting out evil ways. As for your Dharma, who would subject themselves to it?'

The master [Bodhidharma], without rising from his seat, knew from a distance that Spiritual Excellence had fallen from the principle, so he said to Paradhi, 'Spiritual Excellence has departed from my instructions and has secretly preached to the king but he is just about to be humbled. Now be quick and rescue him!'

Paradhi, respectfully receiving the master's instructions, said, 'Would that I could borrow some spiritual strength!' and having spoken a cloud arose under his feet and landing silently he came into the presence of the king.

At that very moment the king was about to put another question to Spiritual Excellence when he suddenly saw Paradhi arriving on a cloud. Flabbergasted, the king forgot his question and said, 'The one who is riding on a cloud, is he good or is he evil?'

Paradhi answered, 'I am neither good nor evil, but come to correct evil. If His Majesty's heart is just, he will regard me free of good and evil.'

The king, although astonished, had a proud, haughty side, which prevailed, so he rejected Spiritual Excellence, ordering him to leave.

Paradhi said, 'Since Your Majesty is possessed of the Way, why expel the monk? While I am without understanding, Your Majesty is welcomed to question me.'

The king was angry, but nevertheless he asked, 'What is Buddha?'

Paradhi answered, 'Seeing into one's own nature is Buddha'.

'Has the teacher seen into this Nature or not?' asked the king.

'I have seen into the Buddha-nature.'

'Where is this Nature?' asked the king.

'The Nature is in its functioning,' responded Paradhi.

'What is this functioning?' asked the king, 'I don't see it at this moment.'

'It is functioning at this moment, though His Majesty himself does not see it,' said Paradhi.

'Is it present in me or not?' demanded the king.

'If it is functioning in His Majesty then he is without fault,' responded Paradhi, 'but if it does not function His Majesty will find it difficult to see into his own essence.'

The king said, 'Whilst functioning where does it manifest?'
'Whilst functioning it has these eight manifestations.' answered Paradhi.
'Tell us of these eight manifestations,' said the king.
Paradhi then recited the following *gatha*:

As foetus it comes to embodiment
The world calls it man
In the eye it is called seeing
In the ear it is called hearing
In the nose it distinguishes smells
In the mouth it talks in discourse
In the hand it seizes and apprehends
In the foot it moves quickly
Manifesting, it is everywhere in the universe
Compressed it is a tiny speck of dust
Aware one knows it is the Buddha-nature
Not being aware of it, it is called spirit-essence.

Having heard this *gatha*, the king's heart was suddenly awakened and, repenting of his former mistakes, inquired tirelessly into the essentials of the Dharma day and night for the length of ninety days.

At that time Spiritual Excellence, being banished, retired into the depths of the mountains and thought to himself, 'I am now already one hundred years old and have spent eighty years in wrong practices and for the last twenty years have taken refuge in the Buddha's Way. Although my nature may be stupid, yet my conduct has been uncompromising towards my faults. Still it has been impossible to guard against these difficulties. Having been born, it were better now to die.' So saying, he threw himself over the precipice. Suddenly a Heavenly Being appeared, caught him up and placed him on a rock, gently and without harming him. Spiritual Essence said, 'I was a humble monk taking the True Dharma as my rule, yet was unable to stop the king's wrong deeds, therefore I offered myself as expiation. What deity has come to help a mere mortal? Things having come to this pass, please let fall a word to comfort me for the rest of my days!'

Whereupon the Heavenly Being recited the following *gatha*:

The Master's long life reaches its hundredth year
In eighty of which he had trained in error.
Perfumed by the desire for cultivation
He had entered the Way
To be near to the Supreme Master.
Although of small knowledge and wisdom
There is much in him of "I" and "other".
Having seen many wise ones
The cherishing of respect has yet to arise.
After twenty years of meritorious conduct
His heart is not yet at peace.
Due to cleverness and disrespect
This situation has now come about
And having won the disrespect of a king
This is the result.
From now on do not be idle
So that within a very short time
The wonderful wisdom will fruit.
All sages live completely from the heart
The Tathāgata also came to this.

Spiritual Excellence was quietly sitting amongst the rocks, joyfully listening to this *gatha*. At the same time the king, with his heretical views, again questioned Paradhi, 'Kind Sir, who served as your master in insight and eloquence?'

Paradhi replied, 'On leaving the home life Tripiṭaka Master Usaba ordained me at the Sala Temple, but Your Great Majesty's paternal uncle, Bodhidharma, was my master.'

Hearing the master's name, the king was for a long time alarmed and said, 'Unworthy, I inherited the throne and took to wrong ways, turning my back on the True [Dharma] and forgetting my honoured uncle!', whereupon he immediately instructed his senior ministers to invite him.

The master [Bodhidharma] then, in company with the king's emissaries, arrived and caused the king to repent of his former faults and listening to the master's admonitions, he wept and excused himself in his presence. He also ordered Spiritual Excellence back from exile, but the chief minister reported to the throne saying, 'Spiritual Excellence, on being banished, threw himself over a precipice and has perished.'

The king said to the master, 'The death of Spiritual Excellence is all due to me. What kind of compassion would it be to allow me to avoid the guilt for this crime!'

'Spiritual Excellence is at this moment sitting in peace and quiet amongst the rocks', said the master, 'just despatch an emissary and he will come.' The king then despatched an emissary to go into the mountains and indeed, there he saw Spiritual Excellence sitting in quiet meditation. On being summoned he said, 'Although deeply humbled by His Majesty's wish, this poor priest has pledged to remain amongst these rocks and waters. Furthermore, there are good and virtuous men in the kingdom who are as numerous as trees in a forest. Bodhidharma is His Majesty's uncle and the master of the six sects, whilst Paradhi is a dragon-elephant in the Dharma. I pray His Majesty will reverence these two sages, with great happiness to the Imperial realm.'

The emissary having yet to return with his report, the master [Bodhidharma] asked the king, 'Does Your Majesty know whether Spiritual Excellence will return or not?'

'It is not yet known', replied the king.

'At the first invitation he will not come.' said master [Bodhidharma], 'but commanding him a second time, he would have to come.'

After a long while the emissary returned and sure enough it was as the aster had said. The master then took his leave of the king by saying, 'Now may [Your Majesty] cultivate virtue well, for within a short time illness will manifest. As for me, I take my leave.'

Seven days later the king indeed became ill and the country's physicians could not effect a cure. Then the high-ranking relatives and senior ministers remembered the master's earlier prediction, so they quickly dispatched an envoy to him, saying, 'The king's illness is critical – please, out of an uncle's compassion, come from afar to save him!'

Then the master, on arriving at the king's palace, asked sympathetically after his illness. By this time Spiritual Excellence, having also received the king's second summons, had left his mountain vastness, whilst Paradhi, long in the king's favour, also came to ask after his health.

Paradhi said, 'What should be done to relieve the king of this suffering?'

The master then had the crown prince pardon criminals and practice compassion for the sake of the king, as well as reverencing the precious community of monks. The crown prince also repented on behalf of the king saying, 'May all my sins be wiped out!' Having repeated this three times the king's sickness took a turn for the better.

His affinity link with China now coming to fruition, the master realised that it was time to leave on his missionary tour. Having first taken leave of his teacher's *stupa* he then said goodbye to friends and students and finally went to the king's palace, where, in an encouraging and comforting tone, he spoke the following words to the king, 'Sire, please make every effort to practice good works and maintain the Three Treasures. I will leave soon [for China] but shall be back within nine years.'

The king, on hearing the master's words, answered him with mixed and tearful feelings saying, 'What crime has our country committed and how auspicious is this land going to be [without your presence]? Oh Uncle, since there is an affinity link it is not for me to block it. Our only wish is that you do not forget the country of your father and mother and that you make a speedy return on dispatching your mission.'

The king had a large vessel fitted out full of valuable things and he himself, at the head of all his personnel, accompanied Bodhidharma to the port of embarkation.

Bodhidharma in China (3.35)

Floating on the ocean deep, summer gave way to winter three times in all before the Master arrived in Nanhai[183] on the 21st day of the 9th month, of the 8th year of the Putong reign period, in the 44th year of the sexagenarian cycle of the Liang Dynasty[184] (527 CE[185]).

Xuangang, the Prefect of Guangzhou, prepared a welcome and informed the Emperor Wu[186] by letter [of Bodhidharma's arrival]. The Emperor, having

[183] On the Pearl River Delta in modern Guangdong, southern China.

[184] Liang Dynasty, 502-557 CE.

[185] The Master's arrival is not a proven historical fact.

[186] Emperor Wu of Liang, 'the Bodhisattva Emperor' (464-549 CE), r. 502-548 CE, was the Chinese equivalent of Emperor Aśoka due to his support of Buddhism throughout his empire, by establishing many temples and places of worship, as well as writing himself on the subject of Buddha's religion, stimulating many translations of Buddhist Sanskrit works and encouraging the growth of the priesthood. See *Beacon Fire and Shooting Star: The Literary Culture of the Liang (502 557)* by Xiaofei Tian. Harvard-Yenching Institute, 2007.

read the report, dispatched an emissary carrying an Imperial mandate of invitation. On the 1ˢᵗ day of the 10ᵗʰ month [Bodhidharma] duly arrived in Jingling.[187]

The Emperor asked [Bodhidharma], 'Since ascending the throne, We have built temples, copied *sutras* and supported monks without number; what is the merit of all this?'[188]

'Absolutely no merit,' replied the master.

'Why no merit?' asked the Emperor.

'These are merely the small fruits of the human and heavenly realms,' replied Bodhidharma, 'they are the defilements of *karma*, like shadows following forms; although they exist they have no reality.'

'What then is real merit?' the Emperor asked.

Bodhidharma answered, 'Pure Wisdom is wonderfully complete, its essence is of itself empty and quiescent; such is merit, not to be sought with worldly means.'

Again the Emperor asked, 'What is the deep meaning of the Noble Truths?'

'Vast, empty, and nothing holy,' said Bodhidharma.

'Who then is before me?' asked the Emperor.

'Not known,' replied the master.

The Emperor did not come to insight then so the master knew that the circumstances were not propitious and on the ninth day of the eleventh month he secretly crossed the Yangzi River going north.

On the twenty-third of the same month he arrived at Loyang.[189] This was in the time of the later Wei dynasty in the reign of Emperor Xiaoming,[190] in the tenth year of the Dahuo reign period.

---

[187] Modern Nanjing in Jiangsu, on the Yangzi River was the capital of the Liang Dynasty of Southern China.

[188] This famous exchange is the subject of the first 'case' in the '*Biyan Lu*' (Records from the Emerald Cliff, often translated as 'The Blue Cliff Records'), a collection of one hundred *kōans* compiled during the Song Dynasty (11-12th. cent. CE); and a fine product of Chinese religious practice.

[189] The capital of the Northern Wei dynasty.

[190] R. 516-528 CE but dates are still a problem in this era. See note 63 above.

Staying at the Shaolin Temple[191] on Mount Song,[192] there he sat in meditation facing a wall, the whole day in silence. People couldn't understand it so they called him 'the wall-gazing *Brahmin*'. At that time there was a monk named Shenguang who was deeply learned and had lived for a long time near Luoyang by the Rivers Yi and Luo. A scholar well read in many books, he could discourse eloquently on the Dark Learning.[193] Sighing frequently, he would say, 'The teachings of Confucius and Laozi take rituals as the Practice and customs as the Rule, whilst in the books of Zhuangzi and The Changes the wonderful principle is still inexhaustible. Now I have heard that a great master, Damo (Bodhidharma), is residing at Shaolin. I must pay a visit to this peerless sage[194] living not so far distant.' Then he went, visiting morning and evening for instruction. Master Damo was always sitting in a dignified posture facing a wall and so Guang heard no teachings nor did he receive any encouragement. Then Guang thought to himself, 'Men of old, on searching the Way, broke their bones to extract the marrow, let their blood flow to help the starving, spread hairs on muddy roads [to allow people to pass], or jumped off cliffs to feed a tiger. In days of old it was still like this, now what kind of a man am I?'

On December 9th of that year a great snow fell, yet Guang resolutely remained standing and didn't even move, so that at daybreak the snow was more than knee-high. The Master, taking pity on Guang, said to him, 'You have been standing in the snow for a long time, what is it that you seek?'

Guang, in desperation, replied, 'Only to wish that the Venerable Sir might exercise compassion by opening the portal to the sweet dew [of the Dharma] and liberate all beings.'

The master replied, 'The supreme and wonderful Way of all the Buddhas can be put into practice only with vast *kalpas* of energetic perseverance in the difficult training and the enduring of the unendurable. So how, with hardly any

---

[191] Founded in 495 CE during the Northern Wei dynasty by Emperor Laowen. Two *li* to the northwest a small hermitage was built in the time of the First Patriarch and in the mountain behind that was a grotto said to have been the place where Bodhidharma sat in meditation for nine years. 'Wall gazing' was also a term for 'sitting in meditation' whilst meditation in action was called 'the four activities'. See further ZGFJS, III: 504.

[192] One of three peaks in modern Henan Province.

[193] A School of Neo-Daoism characterised by a deep concern with ontological problems. See BCC: 87ff and HCP: 168-236.

[194] A technical term in Daoism, the highest of three rankings for a Daoist sage: a man without self. See *Zhuangzi*, chap. 1. Also an old name for a Buddha.

virtue and little knowledge, with a shallow mind and lazy heart, is it possible to wish to practice in the True Vehicle? This would be diligent labour in vain.'

When Guang heard this lesson from the master he secretly took a sword, cut off his own left arm and placed it in front of the master. The master realised then that Guang was a vessel of the Dharma and said, 'All the Buddhas, on first aspiring to the Way, forgot their body for the sake of the Dharma. You, having cut off your arm in front of me today, may also be of such a stamp.' The master then re-named Guang Huike.

Guang said, 'The Dharma-seal of all the Buddhas, may I hear of it?'

'The Dharma-seal of all the Buddhas is not something obtained from men,' replied the master.

'My heart is not yet at peace,' said Guang, 'may the master grant it rest!'

'Bring the Heart to which peace can be granted,' replied the master.

But Guang said, 'Searching for the Heart exhaustively I have been unable to get hold of it.'

'Then I have given peace to your heart,' said Bodhidharma.

Later the Emperor Xiaoming [of the Northern Wei dynasty] heard of the master's extraordinary doings and dispatched an emissary with an Imperial invitation. Three times the invitation was extended but the master did not descend from Shaolin. The Emperor esteemed him the more and bestowed upon him two linen robes, a gold bowl, a silver pitcher, silk cloth and more. The master refused firmly three times but the Emperor's wish prevailed – the master at last accepted the gifts. The devotion of the assembly's monks and laymen deepened from this time on.

After nine years the master already wished to return to the Western Land of India, so he said to his disciples, 'The time has come, so why should not each of you show what you have understood?'

At this time there was a disciple called Daofu who said, 'According to my understanding it is neither to hold on to words nor to abandon words; this is the Way's functioning.'

The master replied, 'You get my skin'.

The nun Zongchi said, 'What I understand now is that it's like Ānanda seeing the Realm of Akshobhya Buddha – once seen, never seen again.'[195]

---

[195] Akshobhya Buddha is the Immovable One whose realm is in the east, opposite Amitābha. A delightful place enjoyed by those who have diligently practiced the Six Pāramitās. DCBT: 293b.

The master said, 'You get my flesh.'

A certain Daoyu said, 'The four great elements are originally empty, the five aggregates without existence and according to my understanding there is not a single Dharma which can be obtained.'

The master said, 'You get my bones'.

Finally Huike bowed reverently, and then remained standing.

The master said to Huike, 'You inherit my marrow,' and turning to him he addressed him thus, 'In days gone by the Tathāgata transmitted the eye of the True Dharma to the Great Master Mahākāśyapā and from him it was repeatedly passed down until it reached me. I now hand it over to you. You should guard and nurture it. Furthermore, I give you the Robe as the faith in the Dharma. Each has a significance which it is proper to know of.'

Huike said, 'Would the master please give a pointer.'

The master replied, 'The inward transmission of the Dharma-seal is to be in accord with [one whose] Heart has verified the Way. The outer transmission, the Robe, will clarify the teachings of the Chan School. Later generations, being faithless and ungrateful, will doubt, consider and contest ever more, saying that I was a man from India, you a son of this Eastern Land, so how could the Dharma be transmitted, how verified? You who are now receiving this Dharma and Robe, when, in the future, the Buddha-dharma will experience difficulties, it will only be necessary to show this Dharma-robe and my transmission *gatha*; these will amount to the means of making the mission activity go without obstacles. Stop with transmitting the Robe two hundred years after my demise, after which the Dharma will spread to every part of the world. Although those who know of the Dharma are many, those who practice it are few: those who talk of the principle are many, who penetrate it, few. Those profoundly in accord [with the principle] and privately bearing witness will be very many, so when you are expounding the Dharma do not belittle the ones not yet awakened. One thought moment can turn the situation round; then it is equal to the attainment of the Origin. Listen to my *gatha*:'

I originally came to this land
To transmit the Dharma and save deluded beings.
When the single flower opens into five petals [196]
Then the fruit will ripen naturally of itself.

[196] The future five schools (houses) of Chan Buddhism in China.

The master continued, 'I have the *Laṅkāvatāra Sutra*[197] in four chapters which is also to be transmitted to you; this is the essential gate to the Tathāgata's teachings on the Heart-ground and makes it possible for all beings to enter awakening. Since arriving here I have already been poisoned five times. I always extracted and examined it and, being placed on the rocks, the rocks split asunder. The reason for leaving Southern India for this Eastern Region was originally due to seeing that the spirit of the Great Vehicle should prevail in Chi prefecture, Shen province and so I sailed the seas and crossed deserts to find a man for the sake of the Dharma. Coming across disturbed people, all seemed like stammering fools. Today, having given you the transmission, my purpose is now fulfilled.'

[Another record says that the master first lived in Shaolin Temple for nine years and gave Dharma guidance to the second patriarch, teaching him the following: 'Stop with all outside connections; inside make the Heart like a wall – without hankerings: then it is possible to enter the Way.' Although Huike could discuss all kinds of principles of the Heart, he was not yet in accord with the nature of the Way. The master (Bodhidharma) only blocked his mistakes but did not discuss the Heart essence of no-thought. Then Huike said to him, 'I have already stopped all *karmic* connections.'

The master replied, 'Have views of permanence and impermanence not arisen then?'

'Not arisen,' replied Huike.

'What verification can be applied to "neither permanent nor impermanent"?' asked the master.

'That it is clearly in constant awareness, so talking about it has nothing to do with it,' said Huike.

'This is the Heart-essence which is handed down by all the Buddhas, there is no doubt about it!' said the master.][198]

After this conversation Bodhidharma went with his disciples to the Temple of the Thousand Sages in Yumen[199] and stayed there for three days. The governor

[197] T. 670, 671 & 672.
[198] Unspecified source.
[199] In modern Shanxi province.

of the city of Qi[200], Yang Xuanzhi[201], who, from his early manhood had loved the Buddhist teachings, came and asked the master, 'In the Western Region of the Five Indias the masters inherited from the Patriarchs generation after generation. What was their teaching?'

The master answered, 'In one who understands the Buddha Heart School, practice and realisation are in accord; this is called "the patriarchal".'

Again Yang Xuanzhi asked, 'Was there something apart from this?'

The master replied, 'To understand the Hearts of others, to know their past and present, not to be intimidated by having or not having, nor attached to any Dharma, to be neither a sage nor a fool, neither deluded nor awake. One who can be as free as this is called a Patriarch.'

Governor Xuan asked further, 'Although your disciple has been devoted to the Three Treasures for many years, the wisdom is clouded and there is still confusion regarding the real principle. Listening to the master's words just now, I still don't know what to do. Would that the master, out of his great compassion, reveal the purport of the teachings!'

The master knew then that the governor was earnest and sincere and so recited the following *gatha* to him:

Even on seeing evil, do not give rise to aversion;
Even on seeing good, do not diligently hoard it.
Neither abandon wisdom nor court foolishness;
Neither cast off delusion nor seek awakening.
Come to the Great Way and then beyond!
Penetrate the Buddha Heart and cross the stream!
If his orbit is neither that of the common man nor the sage –
Gone beyond like this he is called a patriarch.

When Xuan heard this verse, deep feeling mingled with joy, and he said, 'Oh, would that the master remain in the world for a long time guiding living beings!'

---

[200] In Hubei province, in the region of Mount Tiantai.

[201] A famous scholar who, after a visit to the ruins of Luoyang in 547 CE, wrote an evocative account of its Buddhist Temples in their former splendour, having been the capital city of the Northern Wei Dynasty at the beginning of the 6th century, before its downfall. The account also contains much interesting legendary material, all in T. 51, no. 2092. Dates of author unknown. CL:180

But the master replied, 'I shall soon be gone, for it is impossible to remain much longer. There are endless differences in the root nature of beings and there have been many encounters with calamities.'

'Master, I have not yet questioned the persons who have caused you harm,' said Governor Xuan, 'but I shall remove them from you.'

'My transmitting the secrets of the Buddha has furthered those of deluded ways,' replied the Patriarch, 'harming others whilst being in peace oneself, this is surely not the principle.'

Xuan said, 'If the master will not discuss it, how can the strength of the penetrating wisdom and insight be made known?'

The master then could not leave it in mid-air but made a prophecy:

A river boat cleaves the foaming waves
Concentrated heat melts away metal locks
Five entrances will practice together,
Mostly without contentions.

Governor Xuan, on hearing these words, did not understand their purport but silently took them to heart and then respectfully took his leave. That which the master had predicted, although unfathomable at that time, came later to be proved correct.

This was the time that the Wei dynasty honoured Buddhism, so meditation talents were as numerous as trees in a forest. Vinaya Master Guangtong and Tripiṭaka Master Bodhiruci (Liu Zhisan[202]) were regarded as the rarest of them all. These men heard the master (Bodhidharma) expounding on the Way, stressing the teaching of the Heart, but when each debated with him it was like a swarm of bees in a fight. Having stirred the mysterious wind, causing the Dharma to rain down everywhere far and wide, the people were still narrow-minded and stubborn and could not abide profundity. Contesting even amongst themselves, they bore evil intentions, many times poisoning the Patriarch's food. On the sixth of such attempts, the master, because his connections with China were now at an end and the Dharma had been transmitted to an heir, did not attempt to save himself but just sat down in meditation and passed away.

This was on the fifth day of the tenth month in the nineteenth year of the

---

[202] A monk of Northern India who came to Luoyang in 508 CE and translated some thirty works, HCB: 34.

reign period Taihe of the Emperor Xiaoming of the Later Wei dynasty (r. 516-28 CE), corresponding to the 53rd year of the sexagenarian cycle.[203] On the twenty-eighth day of the twelfth month of the same year he was buried at Xiong'er Mountain (in modern Henan Province) and a *stupa* was erected at the Dingling Temple.

Three years later Songyun[204] was sent as envoy to the Western Lands and there he came across the master in the Congling Mountains[205] lightly dancing by, carrying one sandal.

Yun asked him, 'Where is the master going?'

'I'm going to India,' answered the master. He also told Yun, 'Your ruler has already left the world!'

On hearing this Song was uncertain of its meaning but took his leave of the master and returned east. Having arrived home, he wished to report to the Emperor but he had already died and Xiaozhuang had ascended the throne (r. 528-30 CE). Song then reported the business in full, so the Emperor ordered the vault of Bodhidharma to be opened. The grave was indeed found to be empty except for a single leather sandal in the empty coffin. The whole court was amazed and by Imperial orders the sandal was conveyed to the Shaolin Monastery to be venerated there. Later, in the fifteenth year of the Kaiyuan period of the Tang dynasty, corresponding to the 4th year of the sexagenarian cycle (728 CE), one of the faithful stole it from the Huayan Temple on Mount Wutai (in Shanxi) and these days its whereabouts is unknown.

When first Emperor Wu of Liang had met the master the affinity links were not yet propitious. On hearing of his mission to the land of Wei the Emperor himself wished to compose a memorial tablet to the master but he had no leisure for it. Later he heard of the business with Songyun and then succeeded in doing it.

Emperor Taizong (r. 763-779 CE) conferred the posthumous title of 'Fully Enlightened Great Master' on Bodhidharma and named his *stupa* Pure Seeing in his honour. From the time of the news of the master's death in the 53rd year

---

[203] There is some confusion regarding such dates, purporting to correspond to 536 CE approximately.

[204] An official who in 518 was sent by the Empress Dowager, the regent of the Northern Wei dynasty, to India to obtain Buddhist *sutras*. He returned in 522 with 175 Buddhist works. ZGFJS: III:48.

[205] Part of the Himalayan range in the modern province of Xinjiang.

of the sexagenarian cycle of the Wei dynasty (537 CE) until the first year of the Jingde reign period, corresponding to the 41st year of the sexagenarian cycle (1004 CE) four hundred and sixty-seven years have passed.

3.36 Great Master Huike, the Twenty-ninth Patriarch, the Second Chinese Patriarch.

The twenty-ninth Patriarch Huike (487-593 CE) came from Wu Lao (in modern Henan) and his family name was Ji. His father, whose name was Ji,[206] whilst still childless, once came to the following thought, 'My family reverences the good so why be without a fine son?' He prayed for this for a long time until, one night, he felt a strange radiance in the room, due to which his wife conceived. Having waited so long and because of the auspicious omen of light filling the room – they called the child Guang (Radiance). From very young this boy's interests were not those of other children.

Guang became well read in The Book of Odes, The Book of History and in the Daoist Teachings particularly. He had no liking for domestic affairs but loved to roam the hills and streams roundabout. Later he delved into the books of the Buddhists and attained transcendence through his own efforts. Arriving at the Dragon Gate of the Fragrant Mountain Temple in Luoyang (the Northern Capital), he was ordained by Chan Master Baojing, receiving the full precepts at the Yongmu Temple. After that he travelled to all of the Buddhist Monasteries, looking up those who were learned in the *sutras*, for elucidations on works both of the Great Vehicle and those of the Small Vehicle.

At the age of thirty-two he returned to Fragrant Mountain where he sat in meditation the whole day long. After eight years, suddenly, in the silence, he saw a divine being saying to him, 'You will receive the fruit so why remain here? The Great Way is not far away, you should go south.' Guang knew that this was divine intervention and on account of this he adopted the name Shen Guang (Divine Radiance). The next day, his head ached as if pierced by needles, so his teacher wanted to cure him. Then from nowhere a voice was heard saying, 'This is the bones reforming, it is not an ordinary sickness.' Guang then told his teacher the whole business of the divine visitor so that his teacher examined his skull bone and saw that it was like five mountain peaks protruding in all their splendour. 'This is an auspicious sign which will come true,' he

[206]Different character; homophone.

said 'the revelation to go south must mean that Shaolin's great master Bodhidharma is surely to be your teacher.'

Guang accepted the hint and made ready to go to Shaoshi [the mountain on which Shaolin is to be found]. The account of his obtaining of the Dharma and the robe is in Bodhidharma's chapter.

After the presumed transformation and return to the West [of Bodhidharma] from Shaolin the Patriarch [Huike] continued the propagation of the profound teaching, and searched widely for a Dharma-heir. In the second year of the reign period Heavenly Peace of the Northern Qi dynasty (551 CE), a layman of forty just turned up one day without giving his name yet behaving with perfect decorum. He asked the master, 'The disciple's body is entangled in sickness. May the Venerable Sir please absolve my transgressions.'

'Bring your transgressions, then you will be given absolution', said the Master.

After some time the layman returned and said, 'I have searched for the transgressions but couldn't find them.'

'There', said the master, 'I have given you complete absolution from your transgressions. It is fitting now to rely on the Buddha, the Dharma and the Sangha in life.'

'In seeing the Venerable Sir just now, I already understand what the Sangha is but have as yet not understood what Buddha and Dharma are,' replied the layman.

'This Heart is Buddha, this Heart is Dharma; Dharma and Buddha are not two. The Jewel of the Sangha is like this too,' said Master Huike.

The layman said, 'Today for the first time comes the knowledge that the nature of wrongdoing is neither on the outside nor on the inside, nor in the middle. It is the same way in the case of the Heart – Buddha and Dharma are not two.'

The Patriarch regarded the layman as a deep vessel of the Dharma and shaving his head, said, 'This is my treasure, so his name will be Sengcan (monk-gem).' This was on the 18th day of the 3rd month of the third year of the reign period. At the Guangfu Temple he received the precepts and gradually his sickness got better.

Sengcan was Huike's attendant for two years. One day Huike said to him, 'Bodhidharma came from faraway India with the Treasury of the True Eye of the Dharma, which he privately transmitted to me. I now pass it on to you, together with the Robe of Faith. Listen to my *gatha*:'

If there are grounds for a cause in the first place
Then flowers will come to life from the seeds,
But if there are no seeds in the first place
Then no flowers can grow either.

After the Patriarch had transmitted the Dharma and Robe he added, 'You who have received my teaching, it is fitting to live in the depths of the mountains, and not to go on a missionary journey for there might be political difficulties.'

Can replied, 'Would that the Master, having foreknowledge of this, give full information of it!'

But the Master [Huike] said, 'It is not I myself who knows of it; it is a prediction transmitted to Bodhidharma by Prajñātara, which says, "Although there is good fortune in the Heart, there will be misfortune in the world." According to my reckoning it will be during the course of your lifetime. By carefully pondering on this prediction you will not be stricken by any calamities happening in the world. With me too there are *karmic* residues which will come to fruition now, so good journeying and good practice until the time comes for the transmission.'

Having passed on the Dharma, the Patriarch [Huike] then went to Yedu (in present Hebei Prov.) to propagate the Dharma in the most suitable way. When he uttered the single sound of the Dharma the four congregations all converted to Buddhism. Thirty-four years passed in this way, after which he hid his light and covered his tracks, changing his appearance and frequenting wine stalls, butcher's shops and sharing the local gossip or doing manual work. When someone asked him, 'The Master is a man of Dao, why then does he behave in this way?' The master replied, 'This is the Heart with which I am naturally in tune, what business is it of yours?' Again at the Mountain Gate of the Kuangjin Temple in Guancheng Prefecture (modern Henan Prov.), [the Patriarch] discoursed on the peerless Dao and those who listened were as numerous as trees in a forest.

In that temple at the time was a Dharma-master by the name of Bianhe who lectured on the *Nirvāṇa Sutra*, but when Master Huike discoursed on the Dharma the listeners gradually withdrew to join the master. Bianhe could not overcome his anger and began slandering the patriarch to the district magistrate, Zhe Zhunkan. Zhunkan, feeling confused by this evil talk, condemned the master, who submitted happily to the sentence. Those who really understood the matter said that this was a repayment of a debt. This occurred in the master's 107th year, that is, in the reign of the Emperor Wen of the Sui dynasty, on the 16th day of the 3rd month, in the 13th year of the Kai period, corresponding to the fiftieth year of the sexagenarian cycle (593 CE).

(Textual comment: Haoyue Gongfeng once asked the Venerable Changsha Ling, 'An ancient worthy has said, "If one understands the *karmic* obstructions then they are originally empty, but if one does not understand them then one has to repay the debts from previous lives." For example, take the cases of Master Āryasimha and of the 2nd Patriarch, why did they have to repay any debts?'

Changsha said, 'Those great worthies did not understand Original Emptiness.'

The other replied, 'What is Original Emptiness?'

'It is *karmic* obstructions,' said Changsha.

'What are *karmic* obstructions?' countered the other.

'It's Original Emptiness,' said Changsha.

The other was left speechless, so Changsha recited the following *gatha*:

A borrowed existence is originally a non-existence
A borrowed cessation too is non-existent.
The meaning of Nirvāṇa and of debts to repay
Is of one nature without difference.)

Finally the [Second] Patriarch was buried in the Fuyang Prefecture in the Province of Ci (in modern Hebei Prov.), seventy miles to the northeast. Emperor Dezong of the Tang dynasty (r. 780-805 CE) conferred on him the posthumous title of 'Great Patriarchal Chan Master'. From the Patriarch's transformation to the first year of this Jingde period of the Imperial Song dynasty, corresponding to the forty-first year of the sexagenarian cycle, four hundred and thirteen years have passed.

The Collateral Dharma Heirs of the Second Chinese Patriarch Huike

Through Seven Generations, these were Seventeen Persons in All
(Three are mentioned below)

3.37 Chan Master Sengna

Chan Master Sengna's family name was Ma; even when small he was possessed of an extraordinary spirit and was well read in the classics. At the age of twenty-one he lectured on the Book of Rites and the Book of Changes on the Eastern Sea (in modern Shangdong Province). Listeners gathered as in a market place. When he went south to Xiangbo (Henan) a group of students followed him. Having heard the Second Patriarch [Huike] giving a Dharma-talk he, together with ten fellow students, all left the home life. From this time on his hand never again held a writing brush and he fled for always from all worldly books, taking, in pursuance of a monk's training just one robe, one bowl, one sitting cushion and one meal a day.

In pursuance of his training Sengna served Patriarch Huike for a long time. Later he said to Huiman, one of his followers, 'The Seal of the Patriarchal Heart is not a focus on asceticism, which is merely an aid to the Way and nothing more. When there is accord with the Original Heart and it freely manifests the function of the true light, then asceticism is like earth changing into gold. If there is only asceticism and no clear appreciation of the Original Heart whilst still being bound by love and hate, then asceticism is like walking a dangerous road on a black moonless night. The one who strives for the clarity of the Original Heart should examine himself carefully. Before the senses have registered sounds or forms, where is the Heart? Does it exist? Does it not exist? If it has not been degraded to the level of an existent or non-existent thing then the Heart-jewel shines alone, ever illumining the world, without a speck of dust being able to interfere and with never an instant's break in its continuity. Our First Patriarch also passed on the *Laṅkāvatāra Sutra* in four chapters, saying to the Second Patriarch, "I see that in China this is the only *sutra* that can function as the Seal of the Heart. If, Venerable Sir, you take your practice according to this *sutra*, then the liberation of the world will be gained of itself." And the Second Patriarch, whenever bringing one of his Dharma-talks to a close, would say, "After four generations this *sutra* will have become mere words and ideas. What a pity!" I now pass it on to you, it is fitting to guard and cherish it well, take good care not to transmit it to the wrong man!'

Having transmitted this admonition, the master then took to the road, his end unknown.

3.38 Layman Xiang

Layman Xiang lived in retreat deep in a forest, eating from trees and drinking from mountain streams. Early in the Tianbao reign period of the Northern Qi (550-559 CE) he heard of the flourishing mission of the Second Patriarch Huike and wishing to correspond with him, sent a letter of greeting in which he wrote, 'Shadows arise from forms, just as echoes come from sounds. He who tries to get rid of the shadow by confronting his form does not know that the origin of the shadow is the form. He who tries to stop the echo after raising a shout does not know that the root of the echo is in the sound. To try to do away with the afflicting passions by seeking Nirvāṇa is like leaving the form and searching for shadows. Searching for the fruit of Buddhahood apart from living beings is tantamount to searching for echoes before any sound has been produced. Know therefore that ignorance and awakening is one road, that wisdom and foolishness are not different. Names were created from no names and because of these names there arose right and wrong. Principle was created from no principle and from these principles controversies arose. These are imaginary shape-shifters without reality, for what is right, what is wrong? In empty vanities without substance, what can exist, what does not exist? To make known that in gain there is nothing which can be gained, in loss that there is nothing which can be lost – although I have not paid my respects in person [to the Patriarch] never the less to provisionally set down this understanding is done in the humble hope of a reply!'

The Second Patriarch replied with a letter saying, 'The full insights contained in your letter seem all to correspond to the facts and do not differ from the deep principle. Original ignorance takes a precious stone to be a worthless pebble. Suddenly awakened it is seen as being the true jewel. Ignorance and Wisdom are not different and all the ten thousand things are also like this. Taking pity on those disciples of dualistic views, it is mentioned in this letter. Seeing one's own body and that of the Buddha's as not being different, what would be the point of going in search for the dregs of being and non-being?'

The layman, having unrolled the patriarch's letter and performed the ritual of gratitude, quietly treasured the certificate of authentication.

3.39   Chan Master Xiangzhou Huiman

Chan master Huiman of the Longhua Temple in Xiang Province, whose family name was Zhang, was from Ying Yang (a county in modern Henan Prov.). He first met Chan Master Sengna at that temple, and was impressed by his showing of the Buddha's Way, so that he aspired to live a simple life of poverty. Huiman only saved two needles [for repairing his robe], in winter time begged for alms, but in summer even discarded the needles, saying to himself, 'Let the heart be without fear the whole life long, the body without fleas and lice and sleep untroubled by dreams.' He always relied on alms for his food and never spent two consecutive nights in the same place. Shoes he earned by chopping wood whenever he came to a temple.

In the sixteenth year of the reign period Zhenguan (642 CE), near an old tomb in the grounds of Huishan Temple in Luoyang, Master Huiman once experienced a heavy snowstorm. Going into the temple early next morning he saw Chan Master Tankuang, who was surprised and asked the master where he had come from. 'Is there a place where the Dharma comes from?' responded the master.

Kuang had a search made around the temple for his tracks but the snow was everywhere [virgin] and some five feet high. Kuang said, 'This cannot be fathomed.'

Not long after, hearing that there was going to be a census of the Empire's monks drawn up, all of them fled the temples and hid, except the master, who went freely about everywhere with his bowl, without worry or hindrance. Whether he obtained alms or had to move on was all the same to him; he was empty and peaceful. To those who invited him to stay the night he would say, 'If there is no other monk around then I accept your invitation.'

Once, when talking to someone, he said, 'All the Buddhas expounded on the Heart, to make it known that the Heart has no form. So talking repeatedly about the form of the Heart deeply violates the Buddha's meaning. Furthermore, discussion really contradicts the Great Principle.' Therefore he always carried a copy of the *Laṅkāvatāra Sutra* in four chapters, taking this to be the essentials of [the teachings on] the Heart and practiced in accord with it, as transmitted by the venerable ones of former generations. Later the master, still practising the Way, passed away peacefully and in good health at the approximate age of seventy years.

3.40 Great Master Sengcan, the Thirtieth Patriarch, the Third Chinese Patriarch.

It is not known where the Thirtieth Patriarch hailed from. He first had an interview with the Second Patriarch when he was a layman, but having received the Dharma-transmission he retired to the Yuangong Mountains in the province of Shuzhou (N.W. Anwei).

It so happened that Emperor Wu of the Later Zhou dynasty was persecuting the Buddha-dharma, so the master spent more than ten years travelling to and fro between Sigong mountain in Taihu Prefecture and Yuangong mountain, without ever having a permanent place to live or anybody knowing who he was.

In the twelfth year of the Kaihuang reign period (592 CE) of the Sui dynasty, corresponding to the forty-ninth year of the sexagenarian cycle, there was a fourteen year old novice called Daoxin (Faith in the Way) who came to pay his respects to the Third Patriarch, saying, 'Would that the Venerable Monk's compassion allow me to beg for the Dharma gate of Liberation.'

The master replied, 'Who binds you?'

'No one,' responded Daoxin.

'Why seek liberation then?' asked Sengcan.

On hearing this [Dao] Xin had a great awakening. After serving the Patriarch for nine years he was ordained in the province of Ji and kept the precepts with great care. The master often tested him with profound subtlety and, when he knew that the right circumstances had come to fruition, transmitted the Dharma and Robe to him, with the following *gatha*:

Although a flower seed depends on soil
And out of the soil the flower emerges
Yet if there is no man to sow the seed
The flower bed will in no wise produce a flower.

The master also said, 'After Huike had transmitted the Dharma to me he went to Yedu to spread the teaching, remaining there for thirty years. Since he has just died and having you now as heir, why should I stay here?' Then he went to Luofu Mountain (in Guangdong) but after wandering about at leisure for two years he wished to return to his old stamping ground. A month after his return students and others hastened to arrange a great celebration for their benefactor. The master gave a talk on the "Essentials of the Heart" to the four assemblies and during this Dharma-gathering, held under a great tree, the master, standing with palms together, passed away. This was on the 15th day of the 10th month in the 2nd year of the reign period Daye of the Emperor Yang of the Sui dynasty (606 CE), corresponding to the 3rd year of the sexagenarian cycle.

Emperor Xuanzong of the Tang dynasty conferred upon Patriarch Sengcan the posthumous title of 'Chan Master of the Mirror Wisdom' and his *stupa* was called 'Enlightened Quiescence'.

From that time to this, the first year of the Jingde period of the Imperial Song dynasty – corresponding to the forty-first year of the sexagenarian cycle – about four hundred years have passed.

In the beginning of the Tang dynasty the governor of Henan, Lichang, consistently admired the reputation of the [Third] Patriarch and came to a deep appreciation of its import. When, in the Tianbao reign period, corresponding to the twenty-second year of the sexagenarian cycle (745 CE), he came across Master Shenhui [207] at the Heze temple, he asked Shenhui, 'Where is the Third Patriarch buried? Some say that he went into the Luofu Mountains and didn't return, whilst others say that he died in Shangu temple. I do not know which is true.'

Shenhui replied, 'Patriarch Sengcan returned to Shangu temple from Luofu Mountain and just over a month later revealed his Nirvāṇa. Today his grave can be seen in Shuzhou.'

But Lichang did not believe this and when later he was demoted to an assistant prefectural administrator[208] in the province of Shuzhou, he asked the monks of the Shangu temple saying, 'I've heard that the grave of the Third Patriarch is here in this temple – is it true?'

The head monk Huiguan replied, 'Yes, it is.' Overjoyed, Chang and his fellow officials went together to pay homage and opening the tomb undertook the proper religious ceremony for the cremation of a senior priest. Three hundred grains of rainbow coloured *śarīra* relics were obtained, one hundred grains went to a *stupa* to be built from the salary of Lichang himself, one hundred grains were presented to Shenhui of Heze temple as promised and the remaining one hundred grains were taken by Lichang to his own residence in Luoyang, where a feast was later arranged to celebrate it.

---

[207] The master of the future 6th Patriarch, Huineng.
[208] See H:4623

At that feast the Tripiṭaka Master Ghana from India was one of the assembly and Lichang asked him, 'How many Patriarchs of the Chan School were there in India?'

Ghana answered, 'From Mahākāśyapā to Prajñātara there were twenty-seven patriarchs. If the twenty-two patriarchs of the collateral branches from Master Āryasimha through four generations are added, that makes forty-nine patriarchs all told. If we took it from the Seven Buddhas up to [the Third Chinese Patriarch] Sengcan then it would be thirty-seven generations, excluding the collateral branches.'

Lichang also asked the assembly of senior monks, 'I once saw a list of perhaps fifty or more patriarchs, though the collateral branches differed and the relationships of the members of the school were also uncertain, or just their names were wrong. How can these things be verified?' At that time Chan Master Zhiben, a disciple of the Sixth Patriarch, was amongst those assembled. He answered by saying, 'This is because in the beginning of the Later Wei dynasty (5th c. CE) the Buddha-dharma became gradually weaker [through Imperial disfavour]. There was a Śramaṇa by the name of Tanyao, who, in some confusion, made a list written on white silk, recording the names of the patriarchs but whose correct order was already lost. He hid this list inside his robe, which he concealed in a cave. Thirty-five years later, when the Emperor Wencheng ascended the throne (452 CE), the Buddhist Schools prospered once more and Tanyao, famous for his conduct and integrity, was made primate of the whole Empire. Then he called a meeting of all Śramaṇas to discuss the business, described in *A History of the Transmission of the Treasury of the Dharma*.[209] There are small discrepancies in this work, possibly due to fear at the time of recording [the tables]. Then thirteen more years passed, after which time the Emperor ordered the national scholar Huangyuan Zhen, together with Tripiṭaka Master Buddhasena from Northern India, Ji Fuyan and others to once again examine the Sanskrit texts with respect to the doctrines of the various schools and set in order the transmission accurately.'.

---

[209] The text is still extant, see Taisho no. 2058 (N.J. no. 1340) a history of twenty-three Patriarchs from Mahākāśyapā to Āryasimha. For a discussion of this work, a major source for later versions of the patriarchal lineage, see Adamek, MT: 101-110.

3.41 Great Master Daoxin, the Thirty-First Patriarch, the Fourth Chinese Patriarch.

The family name of the Thirty-first Patriarch Daoxin was Sima. For generations they had lived in Henei (modern Henan Province). Later they moved to the Guangji Prefecture in the province of Qi (Hebei).

The master was very unusual even from his birth and when still young admired all the Dharma Gates of Liberation belonging to the *Śūnyatā* School, as if he had studied them in a previous life. After receiving the Patriarchal Transmission his Heart was collected and without sloth; his flanks never touched the sleeping mat for nigh on sixty years.

In the thirteenth year of the Daye reign period of the Sui dynasty (617 CE) the master led his disciples to the province of Ji (modern Jiangxi). There they came to the provincial city whose several thousand inhabitants were suffering from great trepidation for they had already been under siege by brigands for seventy days continuously. The master commiserated with them, teaching them to focus their attention on the *Mohe Boruo* [Great Wisdom (*Sutra*)].[210] What the brigands then beheld on looking over the city parapet seemed to them like a host of superhuman warriors; they said to each other, 'There are some strange beings within this city, better not attack,' and cautiously withdrew.

During the Wude reign period, corresponding to the twenty-first year of the sexagenarian cycle (624 CE), the master wished to return to Qichun and took up residence on Potou Mountain,[211] where disciples gathered like clouds.

One day, travelling on the road to Huangmei Prefecture (in modern Hubei province), the master came across a young boy of a strangely beautiful appearance, an unusual child. 'What is your name?' asked the master.[212]

' "Nature", but not the common nature,' replied the boy.

'What kind of name (Nature) is that?' asked the master.

---

[210] Possibly the *Mahā-Prajñāpāramitā Sutra*, translated by Kumārajīva between 384 – 417 CE, T 8, no. 223.

[211] In Huangmei Prefecture, Hubei province, there are two peaks, the western one of which is called Mount Potou, where Daoxin, the Fourth Patriarch, settled at the Monastery of the True Teaching, often called 'the monastery of the Fourth Patriarch'. The eastern peak was called Mount Pingmao, on which the 'East Mountain Monastery' was established, the place where the Fifth Chan Patriarch, Hongren , settled.

[212] The word-play here revolves around the two characters 'xing', 性 and 姓, 'nature' and 'family-name', which are homophones.

'It is the Buddha-nature,' replied the boy.
'You do not have a surname then?' said the master.
'Because of the [Buddha] Nature being empty,' replied the boy.

The master remained silent, knowing that this was a vessel of the Dharma. He had his attendant go to the boy's house to ask the parents' permission for him to leave the home life. The parents, realising that it had to do with causes in a previous life, had no strong objections and so surrendered him to the master as his disciple, with the name of Hongren (606-674 A.D). Later the master transmitted the Dharma and Robe to him with the following *gatha*:

Flower seeds have latent natures
Potential comes to birth through the earth
When great *karma* and [Buddha] Nature combine
Then out of potential is born the Unborn.

After this, Hongren was given charge of the master's disciples. One day the master (Daoxin) said to the assembly, 'In the Wude reign period (618-626) I was wandering about on Mount Lu and, climbing to the top, saw Mount Potou in the distance. Over the summit was a purple cloud like a parasol and under it a radiant light dividing into six ways. Do you understand or not?' The whole assembly was silent, but Hongren said, 'Is this not another branch of the Buddha-dharma shooting out form the Venerable Sir?'

'Good!' replied Master Daoxin.

Later, in the Zhenguan reign period, corresponding to the 40th year of the sexagenarian cycle, the Emperor Taizong, favourably inclined to Master Daoxin's reputation, wished to pay his respects to the master [in person] and so decreed that he proceed to the capital. But the master, humbly thanking him, declined three times, finally on grounds of ill health. The fourth time an Imperial Emissary was sent for, with the order, 'If he doesn't come forth, bring the head.' When the Emissary arrived at the mountain and notified the master of his instructions, the master stretched out his neck for the blade, his expression dignified. The Emissary thought this a strange thing and reported it back to the throne. The Emperor admired the master all the more, bestowed costly silks upon him and let him have his way.

On the fourth day of the ninth month of the second year of the reign period Yonghui (651 CE) of the Emperor Gaozong, corresponding to the 48th year of the sexagenarian cycle, the master suddenly admonished his disciples saying, 'All Dharmas are completely liberated. Everyone of you should be heedful and spread the teachings for the future.' Having finished speaking he quietly sat down on his sitting cushion and passed away, at the age of seventy-two. On April 8th of the following year the door of his *stupa* opened of itself and the appearance of the master was as when he was alive. After that the disciples didn't dare close the door again.

Emperor Taizong bestowed the posthumous title of 'Chan Master Dayi' (Great Healer) on the master and his *stupa* was called Ciyun (Clouds of Compassion). From the master's passing into ultimate peace till this first year of the Jingde reign period of the Imperial Song Dynasty, corresponding to the 41st year of the sexagenarian cycle (1004 CE), three hundred and fifty-six years have passed.

3.42 Great Master Hongren, the Thirty-Second Patriarch, the Fifth Chinese Patriarch.

Great master Hongren, the thirty-second patriarch, was from Huangmei in the province of Qi (Hubei) and his family name was Zhou. He was born intelligent but once, wandering around as a young man, he came across a wise man who said with a sigh, 'This boy lacks seven of the [thirty-two] signs [of a Buddha] so will not reach Buddhahood.' Later Hongren came across Master Daoxin and, obtaining the Dharma-succession from him, engaged in teaching on Mount Potou.

In the Xianhun reign period (670 – 673 CE) a layman with the family name of Lu and the personal name of Huineng, from Xin province (Guangdong) came to pay his respects. The master asked him, 'Where have you come from?'

'Lingnan,' replied the visitor.

'What is your business?' asked the master.

'Only to become a Buddha,' answered Huineng.

'People from Lingnan don't have the Buddha-Nature so why bother trying for Buddhahood?' said the master.

'A man can be from the north or from the south, but can it be so with the Buddha-nature?' responded Huineng.

The master knew then that this was an unusual man, but scolded him aloud saying, 'To the dormitory with you!'

Huineng bowed respectfully and withdrew. Later he went to the rice-hulling shed, where he worked tirelessly on the rice pestle day and night. Eight months passed and then the master (Hongren) knew that the time for the Transmission of the Dharma had arrived, so he said to his assembly, 'The True Dharma is difficult to fathom and you must not rely on my words, or make them your own. Rather should each one of you write a verse which corresponds to your own understanding and if your words are in profound agreement, then the Robe and Dharma will be transmitted.'

At that time there were more than seven hundred monks in the assembly. The head monk, Shenxiu, learned in both the Buddhist Scriptures and the secular classics, was much respected by all in the community. Everyone praised him saying, 'Who but the Venerable Shenxiu would dare it.' Shenxiu, secretly hearing the high opinion of the assembly and without reflecting further about it, wrote a verse on a corridor wall, which read:

The body is the Bodhi-tree
The Heart like a bright mirror on a stand
Polish it diligently always
Do not allow any dust.

Master Hongren, on passing by and suddenly seeing this *gatha*, knew it was written by Shenxiu and admiring it, said, 'If future generations rely on this for their practice they will surely obtain a superior fruit.' The wall was originally to be used for a painting by Luzhen, a retired scholar-official, of a scene from the *Laṅkāvatāra Sutra*, but when the verse was seen on the wall, the painting was stopped and everyone was ordered to recite it. Huineng, in the rice-hulling shed, suddenly heard the verse being recited and asked a fellow student, 'What are those lines?'

The student replied, 'Don't you know that the master is looking for a Dharma-heir and that he had everyone write a verse from the Heart? This one is written by head monk Shenxiu and the master has praised it deeply, so surely the Dharma and Robe will be transmitted to him.'

Huineng said, 'What does the verse say?'

The student recited it and Huineng, after a long silence said, 'It is a beautiful verse, really beautiful, but its understanding is not complete.'

The student derided him heartily saying, 'What does a common labourer know, don't come out with such idiotic talk!'

'You don't believe me? I want to write a matching verse!' said Huineng. The student didn't answer; then they looked at each other and laughed. When night came Huineng quietly asked a boy to take him to the wall and, himself holding the candle, had the boy write a stanza by the side of Shenxiu's, which read:

Bodhi is not a tree originally
The heart-mirror too is without a stand
Since originally not a thing is
To what avail is removing dust?

After the patriarch Hongren had seen this verse he asked, 'Who composed this? He has not yet seen the [Buddha] Nature either.' When the assembly heard of the master's words they didn't look at this verse anymore.

That night the master secretly sent someone to summon layman Huineng from the rice-hulling shed to come to his room. The master then said this to Huineng, 'All the Buddhas have appeared in the world for the sake of the great matter and have led people according to their capacity, whether great or small; thus the 'ten stages', the 'three vehicles', the 'sudden' and 'gradual' teaching gates and others arose. Now the peerless, wonderful, intimate, completely clear treasury of the Dharma-eye was transmitted consistently over twenty-eight generations until it reached Bodhidharma, who brought the teachings to this land. Then Patriarch Huike obtained the Transmission and Robe and from him they came to me. Now I pass on the Treasure of the Dharma, together with the Robe, to you. Guard them well and do not allow them to perish. Listen to my *gatha*:'

Sentience sows the seed
Due to the ground, the fruit arises.
No sentience, no seed
No nature, also no arising.

Huineng kneeled down to receive the Robe and Dharma and asked, 'The Dharma has been transmitted but to whom should the Robe be given?'

The master answered, 'In former days, when Bodhidharma first came here, men did not yet have faith, so the Robe was transmitted as an unequivocal token that the Dharma had been passed on. Today the faith has already matured in peoples' hearts, which means that the Robe might be a cause for strife, so keep it rather than passing it on. Moreover, you must go far away from here, into hiding, until the time has come to spread the Dharma. As the person who has just received the Transmission and Robe, your life is hanging on a thread!'

Huineng said, 'Where should I go into hiding?'

'Go to Huai [district] for a while,' answered the master, 'then travel to Hui and hide there.'

Huineng, having made the prostrations and in possession of the Robe, withdrew. That night, without anyone in the great assembly knowing of it, he journeyed south. Patriarch Hongren did not ascend the platform for three days. The congregation found this odd and questioned him, but the master replied curtly, 'My teaching has gone so why ask questions about it?'

Again they asked, 'Has someone obtained the Dharma and Robe?'

'Huineng has got them,' said the master.

Then the congregation talked about layman Lu, whose name was also Huineng. They looked for him but he had already gone; then they knew that it was he who had got it, so they all went after him.

Four years after transmitting the Dharma and Robe, in the second year of the reign period Shangyuan (675 CE), Patriarch Hongren suddenly told his congregation, 'My task is now finished. It is time to go.' He then entered his room, sat down quietly and passed away at the age of seventy-four.

His *stupa* was built on East Mountain in the district of Huangmei.

Emperor Taizong conferred upon him the posthumous title of Daman Chan Shi (Chan Master of Great Abundance) and his *stupa* was named Fayu (the Rain of the Dharma).

From the year of the demise of the patriarch until the first year of the Jingde reign period of the Imperial Song Dynasty, corresponding to the 41st year of the sexagenarian cycle (1004 CE), three hundred and thirty years have passed.

End of Book Three

Finding List

for CDL books **1-3** from sources T, XY, FG and DC
(W = W[hitfield] numbering in XY)

bk	W. .	name	Taisho	XY	FG	DC
1	1	毘婆尸佛	204d1	4	18	1
	2	尸棄佛	204d9	6	18	1
	3	毘舍浮佛	205a5	7	19	2
	4	拘留孫佛	205a12	7	19	2
	5	拘那含牟尼佛	205a19	8	20	2
	6	迦葉佛	205a26	9	20	2
	7	釋迦牟尼佛	205b4	10	21	2
	8	第一祖摩訶迦葉	205c22	17	24	3
	9	第二祖阿難	206b7	23	26	4
	10	第三祖商那和修者	206c25	27	29	6
	11	第四祖優波鞠多者	207b1	30	32	6
	12	第五祖提多迦者	207c14	34	34	7
	13	第六祖彌遮迦者	208a16	36	36	8
	14	第七祖婆須蜜者	208b11	38	38	9
	15	第八祖佛陀難提者	208c2	40	39	9
	16	第九祖伏馱蜜多者	209a2	43	42	10
	17	第十祖脅尊者	209a16	44	42	10
	18	第十一祖富那夜奢	209b11	46	44	11
	19	第十二祖馬鳴大士	209c1	48	46	11
	20	第十三祖迦毘摩羅	210a1	51	48	12
	21	第十四祖龍樹尊	210a29	53	50	13
2	22	第十五祖迦那提婆	211b2	59	56	14
	23	第十六祖羅羅多	211c12	63	59	15
	24	第十七祖僧伽難提	212a25	67	61	16
	25	第十八祖伽耶舍多	212c2	70	62	17
	26	第十九祖鳩摩羅多	212c20	72	64	17
	27	第二十祖闍夜多	213a17	74	66	18
	28	第二十一祖婆修盤頭	213b16	77	68	19
	29	第二十二祖摩拏羅	213c19	80	70	20

Bibliography

Select Bibliography of Western Books

Adamek, Wendi L. *The Mystique of Transmission.* New York: Columbia University Press, 2007.

Bol, Peter K. *This Culture of Ours: Intellectual Transitions in T'ang and Sung Culture.* Stanford: Stanford University Press, 1992.

Cahill, Suzanne E. 'Taoism at the Sung Court: The Heavenly Text Affair of 1008', *Bulletin of Sung and Yuan Studies* 16 (1980): 23-44.
Transcendence and Divine Passion: The Queen Mother of the West in Medieval China. Stanford: Stanford University Press, 1993.

Carus, Paul. *History of the Devil.* Open Court, 1900. Reprint: NCY: Land's End Press,1969.

Chaffee, John W. *The Thorny Gates of Learning in Sung China.* Albany: State University of New York, 1995.

Cheetham, E. *Fundamentals of Mainstream Buddhism.* Enfield: Eden Grove Editions, 1996.

Cleary, Thomas and J.C. Cleary, (trans). *The Blue Cliff Record.* 3 vols. Boston: Shambhala, 1977.

Cleary, Thomas, (trans). *The Flower Ornament Scripture.* Boston: Shambhala, 1984.
(trans). *Secrets of the Blue Cliff Record. Zen Comments by Hakuin and Tenkei.* Boston: Shambhala, 2000.

Couliano, I.P. *Out of this World.* Boston: Shambhala, 1991.

Couvreur, Séraphin. *Mémoires sur les Bienséances et les Cérémonies, Tome* II. Leiden: E.J. Brill, 1950.

Davies, Richard L., (trans). *Historical Records of the Five Dynasties.* New York: Columbia University Press, 2004.

Dunnell, Ruth W. *The Great State of White and High: Buddhism and State Formation in Eleventh-Century Xia.* Honolulu: University of Hawaii Press, 1996.

Eliade, Mircea. *Shamanism: Archaic Techniques of Ecstasy.* Harmondsworth: Arkana Penguin Books (reprint), 1989.

Fung Yu-lan. *A History of Chinese Philosophy.* Princeton: Princeton University Press, 1953, 1973.

Gernet, Jacques. *A History of Chinese Civilization.* Cambridge: Cambridge University Press, 1982.
Buddhism in Chinese Society. New York: Columbia University Press, 1995.

Granet, Marcel. *The Religion of the Chinese People.* (1929) Reprint: Oxford: Basil Blackwell, (trans: Maurice Freedman), 1975.

Graves, Robert, and Patai, Raphael. *Hebrew Myths: The Book of Genesis.* New York: Greenwich House, 1983.

Halperin, Mark. *Out of the Cloister: Literati Perspectives on Buddhism in the Song.* Cambridge MA and London: Harvard University Asia Centre, 2006.

Hori, Victor Sogen. *Zen Sand.* Honolulu: University of Hawaii Press, 2003.

Jin Qian, *Formation of the Xikun style Poetry.* Thesis submitted to the University of Massachusetts, 2009.

Kaptchuk, Ted J. *Chinese Medicine: The Web that has no Weaver.* London: Rider, 2000.

Kraft, Kenneth. *Eloquent Zen: Daito and Early Japanese Zen.* Honolulu: University of Hawaii Press, 1992.

Lamotte, Etienne, (trans). *L'Enseignement de Vimalakirti.* Louvain: Catholic University of Louvain, 1962. (re-translated into English by Sarah Boin, Pali Text Society, 1966) *History of Indian Buddhism.* (English trans. Sarah Boin). Louvain: Catholic University of Louvain, 1988.

Lau, D.C., (trans). *Mencius.* Harmondsworth: Penguin Classics, 1970.

Laufer, Berthold. *Sino-Iranica: Chinese Contributions to the History of Civilization in Ancient Iran.* Chicago: Field Museum Press, 1919.
The Prehistory of Aviation. Chicago: Field Museum Press, 1928.

Law, B.C. *Geography of Early Buddhism.* London: Kegan Paul, Trench & Trübner, 1932.

Legge, James, (trans). *The Doctrine of the Mean.* Oxford: Oxford University Press, 1893.

Lu K'uan Yu (Charles Luk). *Chan and Zen Teaching.* First Series. London: Rider, 1960.
Chan and Zen Teaching. Second Series. London: Rider, 1961.

Masson, Jeffrey Moussaieff. *The Oceanic Feeling: Origins of Religious Sentiment in Ancient India.* Dordrecht: Reidel, 1980.

Nakamura, Hajime. *Indian Buddhism.* Delhi: Motilal Banarsidass, 1989.-

Nobel, Johannes, (trans). 'Kumārajīva' in *Sitzungsberichte der Preussischen Akademie der Wissenschaften,* Philosophisch-Historische Klasse, Jahrgang 1927. Berlin, 1927.

Peers, J.C. *Soldiers of the Dragon: Chinese Armies 1500 BCE-1840 CE.* Oxford: Osprey, 2006.

Puri, B.N. *Buddhism in Central Asia.* Delhi: Motilal Banarsidass, 1987.

Robinson, Richard H. *Early Mādhyamika in India and China.* Madison: University of Wisconsin Press, 1967.

Romila, Thapar. *Asoka and the Decline of the Mauryas.* Oxford: Oxford University Press, 1961.

Rotman, Andy, (trans). *Divine Tales: Divyadāna Part I* .Boston: Wisdom publications, 2008.

Schlutter, Morten. *How Zen Became Zen.* Honolulu: University of Hawaii Press, 2008.

Sekida, Katsuki, (trans). *Two Zen Classics.* New York: Weatherhill, 1977; (rprt. 1995).

Sen, Tansen. *Buddhism, Diplomacy, and Trade: The Realignment of Sino-Indian Relations, 600-1400.* Honolulu: University of Hawaii Press, 2003.

Shafer, Edward H. *Mirages on the Sea of Time: The Taoist Poetry of T'sao T'ang.* Berkeley and Los Angeles: University of California Press, 1985.

Singh, Rana P.B. *Where the Buddha Walked: A Companion to the Buddhist Places of India.* Varanasi: Indica Books, 2003.

Strong, John, (trans). *The Legend of King Aśoka.* Delhi: Motilal Banarsidass, 2008.

Tarn, W.W. *The Greeks in Bactria and India.* Cambridge: Cambridge University Press, 1938.

Tatleman, Joel, (trans). *The Heavenly Exploits: Biographies from the Divyāvadāna.* New York: New York University Press, 2005.

Toynbee, Arnold. *A Study of History.* Oxford: Oxford University Press, 12 vols., 1934-61. Rprt. 1979.

Waley, Arthur. *The Analects of Confucius.* London: Allen and Unwin, 1938.

Welter, Albert. *Monks, Rulers, and Literati: The Political Ascendancy of Chan Buddhism.* Oxford: Oxford University Press, 2006.

Wittern, Christian, (trans). *Das Yulu des Chan-Buddhismus: Die Entwicklung vom 8.-11. Jahrhundert am Beispiel des 28. Kapitels des Jingde chuandenglu (1004).* Bern: Peter Lang, 1998.

Jingde chuandenglu. Aufzeichnungen von der Übertragung der Leuchte aus der Ära Jingde. Berlin: Suhrkamp Verlag, 2014.

Wright, Arthur F. and Twitchett, Denis, eds. *Perspectives on the Tang.* New Haven and London: Yale University Press, 1973.

Xiaofei, Tian. *Beacon Fire and Shooting Star: The Literary Culture of the Liang (502-557).* Cambridge MA and London: Harvard-Yenching Institute, 2007.

Yampolsky, Philip B. *The Platform Sutra of the Sixth Patriarch.* New York: Columbia University Press, 1967.

Young, Stuart H. *Conceiving the Indian Buddhist Patriarchs in China.* Michigan: Ann Abor, 2008.

Zürcher, E. *The Buddhist Conquest of China.* Leiden: E.J Brill, 1972.

Index

CPSIA information can be obtained
at www.ICGtesting.com
Printed in the USA
LVHW041924120120
643360LV00004B/479/P

9 783738 662467